PERIOD GARDENS

Myles Baldwin

Period Gardens

Landscapes for Houses with History

PHOTOGRAPHY BY SIMON GRIFFITHS

MURDOCH BOOKS

I would like to dedicate this book to my mother, Julie

CONTENTS

INTRODUCTION 6

APPROACHING PERIOD DESIGN 14

HISTORY 20

RENAISSANCE 36
    LA FOCE 40

JACOBEAN (LANDSCAPE) 54
    STOURHEAD 58

GEORGIAN (PICTURESQUE) 72
    HASELEY COURT 76

VICTORIAN (GARDENESQUE) 86
    RONA 90
    BRONTE HOUSE 104

EDWARDIAN (ARTS AND CRAFTS) ... 120
    HODGES BARN 124
    INGLENEUK 136
    ROFFORD MANOR 146
    MOIDART 158

SPANISH MISSION 168
    BOOMERANG 172

HOMESTEAD 186
    CRUDEN FARM 190
    COMFORT HILL 202

ART DECO AND MODERNIST 212
    WYLDEFEL GARDENS 216

DETAILS 228
    LAWNS AND TENNIS COURTS 232
    PAVING 236
    PATHS 238
    DRIVES 240
    POOLS 242
    PONDS 244
    WALLS, FENCES AND HEDGES ... 246

BIBLIOGRAPHY 250

INDEX 252

INTRODUCTION

Having received my early training at one of Australia's oldest gardens and grandest houses, history and architecture have always played a major role in my approach to landscapes.

MY FIRST 'REAL JOB' was at Sydney's Royal Botanic Gardens, where I was lucky enough to be accepted to do an apprenticeship in horticulture. I do mean lucky – at the time of my induction, more than 200 school leavers, mature-age students and professional gardeners had applied for the job. Armed with my high school leaving certificate and some photographs of a small fern garden I had made two years earlier for my parents at our home in Sydney's south, I was ready for my interview.

My mother drove me to the Gardens' head office on Mrs Macquarie's Road and ducked around the corner to wait. The old building that once served as the curator's residence and hub of horticulture had been remarkably well preserved and had a new lease of life as a historical feature, while the rest of plant sciences and administration of the gardens was left to a newer modern annexe. I met Andrew McCartney, the apprentice liaison officer and one of the nicest people in horticulture, who walked me through the naphthalene-filled lower floor of what I found out later was the herbarium, across a skywalk and into a room in the adjacent Maiden building.

My interview was short, but felt like it went for an eternity. I was nervous and even managed to spill my glass of water on the table. In the room were Bruce Rann, the then curator of outdoor collections, and Debbie Pinches, who was in charge of personnel. They probably interviewed dozens of people that day, and every time it was most likely the same questions: 'Why would you like to work here?' and 'What have you got that will make us want to employ you?' Admittedly, I probably gave the same answers as everyone else that day, but the one advantage I hoped I had over the others was a passion for gardening, and for me

to succeed in the one career I wanted to do, I needed the Royal Botanic Gardens.

The photos I showed them told the story. The fern garden I had made for my parents was originally a dead lawn and soil mound under a large jacaranda. By levelling this space and using multiple plantings of *Cyathea australis* (rough tree fern) and *Asplenium nidus* (bird's nest fern), I created what I now call a thematic garden. I then grew pteris and blechnum ferns to support the major foliage and for accent planting. I collected begonias to rise up through the lower foliage, adding colour and

time to be at the gardens. Sydney was well into preparation for the 2000 Olympics and government grants to major harbourside attractions like the RBG and greater Domain meant that projects could be tackled on a scale that may never be repeated.

My first posting as an apprentice was significant – I was positioned on the Government House gardening division. Gordon Samuels had been appointed Governor of New South Wales in 1996 and was the first not to be resident at Government House. Not only was it a break in tradition

My time at the Royal Botanic Gardens opened my eyes to the widest diversity and experience a young gardener could hope for. Every facet of horticulture, arboriculture, landscaping and garden design could be met and challenged. It was also an exciting time to be at the gardens. Sydney was well into preparation for the 2000 Olympics.

height where required. The garden also needed to be accessible, and I collected pavers from an old pile in the backyard. After compacting and levelling a layer of sand with a block of wood, I laid the pavers in a stretcher bond pattern, parallel to the house. As I didn't have a brick saw, the pavers were left with a toothed finish, which I disguised with the trendy plant of the moment, mondo grass (*Ophiopogon japonicus*). Not bad for a teenager with no experience in garden construction. A week after the interview, a phone call changed my life.

My time at the Royal Botanic Gardens (RBG) opened my eyes to the widest diversity and experience a young gardener could hope for. Every facet of horticulture, arboriculture, landscaping and garden design could be met and challenged. It was also an exciting

but, in garden terms, it was the first time the property could be approached from a purely horticultural direction rather than one dictated by the whims of the Governor's household.

Vice-regal functions were the deadlines ruling the property, which is run by the Governor's office along with the Historic Houses Trust of New South Wales. Everything needed to be kept shipshape. On one or two instances my job was even to vacuum the lawn.

Planting wise, the design and evolution of the garden was left up to senior horticulturalist Martin Zierholz. Martin's horticultural knowledge and talents far exceeded those of any gardener I had ever met. Born and trained near the Black Forest in Germany, he had an encyclopaedic knowledge of cooler climate perennials and propagation, and was experienced in the creation of large-scale perennial borders. With his knowledge of plants, he was able to understand how they would fill out a bed, what colours would suit, and also be able to propagate them to create a perpetual garden.

The garden was divided up into three areas – the parade lawn, and the eastern and western terraces. All guests entered past the parade lawn, via the carriageway. Annual beds flanked the bitumen drive, with masses of bold, almost gaudy, colour. So bright were these gardens that they are burnt into my memory. Variegated flax was planted at either end of the garden beds, *Amaranthus tricolor* 'Joseph's Coat' filled the central areas and the border was planted with *Gomphrena globosa*. I thought the whole arrangement was shocking, as my own personal tastes about colour and arrangement had not matured, and my scant knowledge of history prevented me from seeing that this was a significant part of Victorian garden design.

Adjacent to the entry was the western terrace, then a failed rose garden, which in its heyday had been one of the most beautiful landscapes in the country. The garden itself was merely an arboretum, but was home to many of the more desirable plants of the time. Various species of araucaria grew beside coral trees, poplars and figs. A romantic path of compacted earth and crushed stone meandered through it, creating a circuit that would have been used for displaying the collection. It was a typical Landscape-style garden with a Gardenesque influence.

An arboretum was a significant part of all large Victorian gardens. It provided a retreat from the heat in warmer climates and was a display of the extent of one's travels, or boasting rights of one's horticultural prowess.

In my last six months at the RBG, I expressed an interest in design and started

PREVIOUS PAGES: the eastern terrace of Government House, planted with teucrium, New Zealand flax, day lilies and ensete bananas.
This page: Royal Botanic Gardens' employee on the eastern terrace of Government House.

View of Sydney Harbour from the eastern terrace of Government House, which is planted with society garlic, New Zealand flax, miscanthus, *Salvia leucantha* and agapanthus. A New Caledonian pine stands in the background.

working with the garden's senior landscape architect, Ian Innes. One of his projects was the reinstatement of the western terrace and significant historic features at Government House. In the RBG's historic records library, we managed to piece together, using early photographs, drawings and lithographs, the location of many of the larger specimens used, plus the layout of the meandering path. The garden had reached its peak in the 1870s and was later removed due to changing fashions, high maintenance and the whims of governors who wished to modernise the property.

The focal point of Government House was the perennial garden on the eastern terrace. Receiving many facelifts over the years as governors came and went, this garden was used primarily for entertaining, as it was accessible from the public rooms. It is a basic design of a large flat lawn bisected like a St George Cross with stone paths, and with a pond at the intersecting point. The premier features in the design were the four large perennial gardens that ran along the east–west axis away from the stately building. Martin Zierholz had been working the beds for two years before I saw them, and had managed to achieve perennial perfection. Overall, the gardens appeared to be evenly planted with matching colour schemes, a mirror of one another, heading away from the house. On closer inspection, there was much more. First, the further the gardens were from the house, the larger the drifts of plants and the less detail, which meant that, viewed from the house, the gardens would appear to have a consistency of detail and impact.

The random nature of the gardens was also an illusion, and actually relied upon the perfect spacing of repetitive focal points and vertical accents. Each of the beds used thick clumps of *Phormium tenax* 'Variegatum' (variegated flax) which was then supported by large clumps of *Canna iridiflora* and two species of salvia. By keeping within the confines of these four plant species to form the basis of the garden, additional plantings were added, but used as accent plantings and for additional seasonal colour. At any one time, there may have been 20 species per bed, but always with a dominant grouping within. Each bed was also a good 4 metres deep and 15 metres long (13 feet by 49 feet), the size and scale perfect for such a broad open landscape and long vista.

I learnt at Government House not to worry about small gaps when planting perennial borders – you just need to be sure that plant groupings are proportionately the right size. That way, the smaller gaps will disappear. Overcrowding a perennial garden can be as big a mistake as underplanting one.

Other gardens at Government House included the outer shrubbery borders, which contained spectacular plantings with broad leaves and contrasting colour, designed to be seen from a distance. My favourite combination plantings were the vibrant *Acalypha wilkesiana* (Fijian fire plant) intertwined with philodendron and *Strelitzia nicolai* (giant bird of paradise), and the *Yucca filamentosa* grouped with *Hymenocallis caribaea* (spider lily). The spring walk was also an interesting part of the garden to work in, but seemed somewhat out of place, surrounded by oleanders and phoenix palms. Pink *Prunus cerasifera* 'Nigra' (purple leaf flowering plum), may bush and crocus were made insignificant by bolder tropical foliage and, to me, a garden developed around the concept of being entertaining for two weeks of the year is a waste of time.

I returned to work at Government House several times throughout my apprenticeship, both as a gardener and, for 12 months, as the florist for vice-regal functions. (It's a long story.) The RBG also had me working in the rose garden, as part of the landscaping team, in the historic middle gardens, and on bush regeneration in the Domain district. Sadly, at the end of 2000, my time at the RBG was ending and I needed to find a job.

Originally, I investigated the idea of working with a design company. This proved more difficult than I had expected. It wasn't that jobs weren't available but, rather, that I had been spoilt in my apprenticeship, exposed to horticulture, design and history in an amalgamation that cannot be found in the world of the commercial garden design studio.

Sydney, at the time, was also at the tail end of a rather boring episode in design. Green and white gardens dominated the landscaping industry, with one of the most common abominations being iceberg roses and buxus hedging. It had nothing to do with where I had spent the previous four years. Not impressed with the employment situation, I went north with my family for a January vacation. While contemplating my options on a Queensland beach, I received a phone call. The man on the end of the line said his name was Leo Schofield, that he had heard good reviews of my work at the RBG, and was wondering if I could see him at his garden at Bronte House.

I can be there in a week, I replied, and then asked where Bronte House was.

Looking back, it was a funny thing to say, as Bronte House and the suburb of Bronte were to become the centre of my professional world and still remain so to this day.

APPROACHING PERIOD DESIGN

In creating a period style garden, it's important to draw references from the surrounding architecture and take note of the immediate and regional environment.

A PERIOD GARDEN is a garden that can be dated to an era in design. The garden at the palace of Versailles is a perfect example of architecture matched by a garden design displaying all the traits of the then popular Renaissance landscape movement. A period garden, however, need not be as important, as old or anywhere near as grand as Versailles. It can be the stark, cement-filled landscape of an Art Deco house, an exotic garden around a Spanish Mission house or the overcrowded surrounds of an Arts and Crafts house.

Whether or not the landscape is to the taste of the designer does not matter. To me, a great designer of gardens is one who can look past their own tastes and draw upon their design talents in the uses of space, materials, colour and textures to create the appropriate landscape. This is an essential attribute but one often overlooked in an industry now dominated by gimmicks and the prospect of an instant garden. Many landscape designers have a particular style which they are employed to adapt to any given garden. This may be a brilliant marketing tool, but is not useful for period style works, and is also a little boring, if you ask me.

A period style garden, on the other hand, is designed to reflect the architecture of the residence and its surroundings. The garden need not be a historical re-creation of what was once there, but should be designed to be in keeping with thematic planning as an overall aesthetic. Some research is often required, and a good knowledge of architectural history, art and gardening will be useful.

The key points in designing a period garden also apply to any landscape. First, it's vital not to be caught up in fashion, as that will be out of fashion before you know it. The setting and surrounding architecture are important in all gardens, as are the regional and immediate environments. Most important of all, though, is the owner of the property, without whom no garden would exist.

ARCHITECTURE

When designing a period style garden, architecture is the most significant element and the basis from which to theme the garden.

Some styles of architecture can be easy to spot, but it helps if there is some documentation about the property so that research can be carried out. If the property has little available information, researching the architect (if you know who that is) and the period will allow you to compare other properties of a similar era or by that designer. However, within each period there are often quirks and design idiosyncrasies that make each house unique.

For instance, the architect of Bronte House, Mortimer Lewis, designed the building in a Gothic revival style popular during the mid-1800s. Details such as arched timber cut-outs along the balcony, fine balcony posts, decorative turrets and crenellations are classic features of this style. The house, with its long, low verandas, also has the lightweight feel of a maritime cottage. Although it is the period of the overall architecture that sets the theme for the garden, I have found that it is often the smaller details that will give me ideas for creating a garden with a truly unique setting. Leo Schofield, who was living at Bronte House at the time, noted the ambience of the house

Detail of the tracery on the very rare *Agave victoriae-reginae*, known as the collectors' agave and named after Queen Victoria, near the conservatory at Government House in Sydney.

as a combination of masculine Gothic details with a delicate cottage atmosphere, a blend perfectly suited to a garden that was both bold and highly detailed.

It is these architectural features that dictate how further elements of a garden need to be designed and constructed. Pavilions and pergolas can use similar timberwork, and posts and stonework can be matched for a seamless blend between old and new. The well-known Sydney architect Leslie Wilkinson used stucco walls, plaster friezes and twin columns in many of his colonial Mediterranean designs. Such obvious signatures can simply be lifted and replicated in the landscape. This duplication of architectural elements in the garden is a simple way of beginning a period style design. Essentially, your materials are already set for you and it is only the way you arrange them that requires skill. This is often a good starting point for anyone with great spatial awareness but no great creative flair.

However, construction methods may need to differ, as occupational health and safety and engineering requirements have changed vastly over the years, with the safety of the worker and the cost of insurance seeing the creation of residential gardens moving from a cottage industry to a profession. Such a phenomenon is particularly evident in one of the most basic elements, the retaining wall. Historically constructed from paddock boulders, clay bricks or milled stone, a wall was once simply a matter of basic materials and labour. If the labour was there, the wall was built. Today, most walls over the height of 900mm (3 feet) need to be engineered and require council approval. Solid walls have made way for structural cores with decorative façades. Although the technology is there to build

bigger and better things, it is not often that such commissions are handed out. Whether or not this is because of the bureaucratic jump rope or whether it's a simple case of money and manpower, I'm not sure, but a large walling commission is not what it used to be.

On the plus side, the technological advances that have seen a change in the landscape market are better for the environment and prolong the life of any structure. The main clue for a landscaper of the future trying to decipher whether a garden is heritage or faux heritage probably won't be the material of the wall, but whether or not it's standing upright.

The scale of the garden needs to reflect the architecture and scale of the house. A small hamlet cottage in Somerset need not have sweeping vistas and grand spaces, but would be more suited to shorter, interrupted garden rooms and accessible focal points. This is where design gets a little tricky. Although you may use elements of design from the existing architecture, a desire for particular landscape features is often difficult to control. I have always said that I don't always like what I have to work with, and certain materials may not be to my own personal taste. In period style design, prejudices and personal tastes need to take a back seat in order to achieve a landscape that works.

David Hicks' last garden in the Cotswolds is a case in point. The garden and its layout are impeccable, with the design of the hedges, its formal symmetrical structure and the grandness of the greater vista very impressive features. But it's not what I would have done in that situation. To me, the garden seems over-scaled, claustrophobic in some places and, dare I say, doesn't relate to the house. I'm sure

Mr Hicks was aware of this and most likely didn't care, for he had a different agenda and wouldn't have been interested in my garden theory. There is no denying the greatness of the man; like all great interior designers, he was a master of smoke and mirrors and the quaint little house has been elevated to legendary status. I feel uncomfortable in the pleached hedge avenues, but they frame views from main rooms in the house, where they can be appreciated to greater effect.

An interesting feature about very old houses is that sometimes, like the garden,

to a 0.3 hectare (¾ acre) block in 1979 under the direction of the New South Wales Historic Houses Trust. The goal for the design is obviously not to restore a garden that can never be, but to use the twisted history to create a garden that tells the story, reinforcing the remaining architecture and, to compensate for what was lost, layering something new onto it.

ENVIRONMENT

The environment consists of both macro and micro elements, which can affect the long-term viability of a period works. The environment

die and evolve. That is a fact of life: a garden is not a static element like a museum, but a living thing, which cannot be kept in a glass jar.

With this in mind, although the original architecture and garden layout may state that a lawn or particular garden was to be positioned in one location, it is not required to be reconstructed that way unless appropriate now.

The cloister garden at Boomerang (page 172) is a rare example of a salvageable garden. Constructed in the 1920s, it is a tennis court-sized open space, encircled by a breezeway (or cloister) on the western side of a Spanish Mission house. Originally designed by Max Shelley, the garden was made from sandstone with a Moorish pattern of symmetrical sandstone-flagged paths. The gardens were originally planted with bananas, perennials and roses, an odd combination, but one inspired by Islamic Mediterranean style. Such planting, however, did not sit well with the owners, and the garden was replanted several months after its construction. In the 1980s, when the property left the family's ownership, the cloister gardens were filled in and the area left as a paved space for entertaining. In 2006, under the direction of new owners, the gardens once more received a makeover. Although much of the rest of the property had a new shadier environment, with its own microclimate which needed to be taken into account, that wasn't the case with the cloister, which could be approached in a more archaeological way. Being an area originally of perennials and hard surfaces, there was no concern about large trees interfering and, with no change to the surrounding buildings, light and aspect remained the same. This is the first garden I have ever come across that could be completely restored to its original intent.

The scale of the garden needs to reflect the architecture and scale of the house. A small hamlet cottage in Somerset need not have sweeping vistas and grand spaces, but would be more suited to shorter, interrupted garden rooms and accessible focal points.

they evolve over time, leaving the would-be archaeologist in a fuss. For a period style, however, such a crossing-over of eras only makes the design process more appealing. I love a good story, and a house that evolves will often tell one. A current project of mine is the design and construction of a garden for Lyndhurst, once the home of New South Wales (Australia) principal Colonial Surgeon Dr James Bowman. A magnificent maritime Georgian house, built in 1833, that once laid claim to 14.5 hectares (36 acres), Lyndhurst had a chequered past of bankruptcy, misuse, abandonment and subdivision. Prior to the property's heritage protection, it had been a Catholic school, a laundry, three separate residences, a cabinetmaker's workshop, an ice-cream factory, a broom factory and a printing works. The once waterfront estate was reduced to a mere terrace, only reverting

as a whole in a garden may undergo a few changes in the future as the global climate shifts and we are forced to reassess designs based upon plant survival. But we are not there yet and the environment of a garden usually refers to the immediate confines of the landscape. The immediate environment of a period house is almost guaranteed to have changed since the original inception of the garden. Trees will have emerged on open sunny lawns, hedges will have died, and once great clumps may now be dispersed across the garden. The dynamics of plant life make it virtually impossible to re-create exactly what the original design intent was and, in my opinion, it is a waste of time to attempt such a task. What the historians and purists need to understand is that even from the original design intent any good horticulturalist would know that a garden is dynamic. Plants grow,

Old stones from the conservatory have been reused to make a set of steps at Bronte House in Sydney.
The pathway is planted with an unusual mix of plectranthus and mondo grass.

Part of the reason it's usually so difficult to re-create a garden is that external elements have an enormous impact. Boomerang, for instance, is in an inner-city suburb once made up of enormous houses, but now the most densely populated area in Australia. Over the years, houses have been demolished and gardens subdivided to make way for apartments, and this has had an effect on Boomerang's garden. For a start, the design of the garden has had to change to accommodate additional shade from nearby multi-storey buildings. With more concrete, the surrounding area has become hotter, which needed to be taken into account when planning the garden. With more cars and people around, the effect of noise also has to be considered.

Similar changes have been encountered at Cruden Farm, Dame Elisabeth Murdoch's property (page 190). When the garden was developed almost 80 years ago, it was in a rural setting, and designed with that environment in mind. Now, a four-lane highway runs in front of the house and suburbia has crept within view of the boundaries. That alone reinforces the idea that it makes no sense to slavishly re-create a garden – of course, the original garden can be used as inspiration and expanded upon, but current conditions and requirements need to be a major part of the equation.

On another level – and something that affects everyone involved in period gardens – are the cultural and economic changes that have occurred over the generations. When gardens were constructed decades or even centuries ago, the most expensive element was often the stone and other materials, while labour was extremely cheap (or sometimes free). There's been a complete about-turn in that regard – for example, with modern technological methods for extracting stone, materials are relatively cheaper than they used to be. The cost of building and maintaining a period garden, however, has increased enormously, with the cost of wages, workers' compensation, insurance and other boring facts of life. It means a period garden is harder to do than ever before but it is still, in my mind, well worth the effort.

It takes a special person to want to tackle a garden in a heritage property, with the underlying assumption that it be designed to support the architecture rather than the whims of modern fashion. During work on my second great garden, at Rona (page 90), I was fortunate to befriend owner John Schaeffer, a businessman and philanthropic art enthusiast. It was a learning curve for both parties: on the one hand, for a man who wanted to preserve

The cost of building and maintaining a period garden has increased enormously, with the cost of wages, workers' compensation, insurance and other boring facts of life. It means a period garden is harder to do than ever before but it is still, in my mind, well worth the effort.

THE OWNER

Of course, in my business, nothing is possible without the owner. A great garden has always been a collaboration between gardener and owner, with the relationship forming a horticultural marriage. Strangely enough, as in a marriage, money and communication breakdown are often the causes of rifts between the two parties, resulting in something for better or worse for the garden.

My own partnership with Leo Schofield at Bronte House (page 104) taught me the trials and tribulations of creating a great garden. Fortunately, horticultural knowledge was a forte of Mr Schofield's and the awkwardness of explaining the reasoning behind my actions was not required. In many cases, however, the limited knowledge of the owner has made the inception of a great garden difficult, to say the least. It's not a one-way street, though, and the stubbornness and even arrogance of some gardeners has thwarted just as many partnerships before they got off the ground.

his privacy and views but knew the garden needed to be reworked, and on the other, a gardener who wanted to enforce his own ideals of colour and movement. There was vigorous discussion during the process but, in the end, the garden was the winner, becoming one of Sydney's best specimen garden landscapes.

Another great gardening duo is Dame Elisabeth Murdoch and gardener of 35 years, Michael Morrison. The pair has laboured through drought and storms to develop the magnificent property that exists today. It's a relationship that works brilliantly, with Michael, a stickler for cleanliness, knowing exactly how the garden should be kept and Dame Elisabeth acting as the creative driving force behind it.

But, ultimately, recognition has to go to the property owner. And so it should, for even if the owner is not a gardener, the property belongs to them, they have a dream for it and, as a gardener, it is an enormous privilege to become part of that vision.

HISTORY

For thousands of years, man and nature have worked together to create gardens for many different purposes, from symbols of power to idealised versions of the world.

APART FROM A certain garden of biblical fame, it's impossible to know when or where the first garden was made. In its most basic form, it was probably around 10,000 BC and, rather than being the site of temptation, was simply an area fenced off to protect our ancestors from savage beasts and unfriendly neighbours. Over the centuries, that area was used for growing crops and raising animals and, eventually, as a place to relax, contemplate nature and even, for some, to enjoy the actual feat of creating and looking after the garden itself.

There's nothing that spells out 'civilisation' more than a garden. It's a domain in which humans and nature work together to create an idealised, personal and miniature version of the world and can only be a priority during relatively calm times and within an organised society. The first place on Earth to have reached a stage where gardens were feasible was the Nile, around 4000 years ago. Of course, no gardens from this period have survived, and any knowledge we have of them comes from stylised drawings on tomb walls. From those drawings, you can decipher gardens with ponds, used for irrigation, for cooling and for purely aesthetic reasons; fish in the pond were a source of food and entertainment as well as a way of keeping insect larvae in check. Trees were planted for shade and some, like the olive and date, for food; herbs were grown for culinary and medicinal purposes; and flowers for their beauty and perfume.

Subsequently, gardens sprang up in Mesopotamia, between the rivers Tigris and Euphrates, in an area that is now part of Iraq, and later in Greece and Rome.

Very little is known about Greek gardens, partly because so little painting of the time has survived and also because there was constant rebuilding in Greek towns. However, there is the belief that Roman gardens couldn't have existed without their forerunners in Greece, and there are references in Homer's *Odyssey* and *Iliad* to gardens, groves, forests and courtyards. For instance in Book VII of the *Odyssey*, he writes: 'Outside the gate of the outer court there is a large garden of about four acres with a wall all round it. It is full of beautiful trees – pears, pomegranates, and the most delicious apples. There are luscious figs also, and olives in full growth…In the furthest part of the ground there are beautifully arranged beds of flowers that are in bloom all the year round. Two streams go through it, the one turned in ducts throughout the whole garden, while the other is carried under the ground of the outer court to the house itself…'

The Romans took up much of Greek culture, including religion, art and architecture. Whether there really was anything of Greek gardens to adopt, it's hard to say but, in any case, Romans took to

doubling as outdoor rooms, accessed via colonnaded walkways. Some larger gardens really did try to imitate nature, with lakes, groves and glades along with various buildings, statues and shrines, while others were more along the lines of sculpture grounds and pleasure parks.

ON THE SILK ROAD
And, as for the gardens in Mesopotamia, they were quite different from and much grander than the Egyptian, Greek and Roman ones, being essentially hunting parks and, some, even early incarnations of botanical gardens, planted with specimens collected on travels, as well as flowers and water features. The most famous garden, possibly of all time, is the Hanging Garden of Babylon (which may, or may not, have been in Nineveh rather than Babylon). This was a walled enclosure, built on a hillside, made up of a series of pavilions and stepped boxes separated by cascading water, and planted with trees, flowers and, ripe for the plucking, fruit and vegetables.

The Romans took to gardening with enthusiasm and spread the cult throughout Europe, making gardens wherever they settled and developing their own vocabulary along the way.

gardening with enthusiasm and spread the cult throughout Europe, making gardens wherever they settled and developing a vocabulary along the way. Topiary, for instance, comes from the Latin word *topiarius*, meaning someone employed in an ornamental garden.

As with many aspects of ancient Roman culture, their design of gardens was incredibly sophisticated and modern, with courtyards decorated with fountains and flower beds,

This may have been the most well-known garden, but was one of many, as the whole art of gardens took off in the region. Persia, for instance, was on the Silk Road and absorbed influences from as far away as Greece and India. Its walled, geometrically planned gardens, with elaborate water features, often included pavilions and small temples, and became places for outdoor entertainment as well as for sleeping on hot nights.

Being on the Silk Road had its benefits, but also its difficulties, with Persia on the frontline for invading armies. However, among the spoils taken home by the Arab and Mongolian conquerors were garden plans and, so, a love for outdoor spaces spread further yet, to Saudi Arabia and then, with the spread of Islam, off to other parts of the Middle East, Turkey, Islamic Spain, North Africa, Afghanistan, India and Pakistan. The Koran describes paradise as a garden with four rivers (of water, wine, milk and honey), and influenced the design of the typically Islamic *chahar bagh* walled rectangular garden, divided into four parts, signifying earth, water, fire and air, by water channels. These paradise gardens ranged from tiny courtyards within buildings to sprawling encampments in the country. And, like their forerunners in Persia, Islamic gardens, filled with fruit, scented flowers and even small animals, were used for relaxation, entertaining and, on hot nights, for sleeping. An excellent example of an Islamic garden is at the Alhambra in Granada, Spain, which was built in the fourteenth century – an oasis in an arid location. While enormous, it has been divided into small, walled enclosures, beautifully proportioned, with pavilions, arched galleries, high walls and extraordinary water features. It's one of the most spectacular gardens ever built and for this reason – and also because of its accessibility to the rest of Europe – it has had, and continues to have, enormous influence on landscape design.

At the same time Islamic gardens were springing up, gardens of a different kind were being created in Japan and China. These were more stylised than their Islamic counterparts, linked very closely with poetry, philosophy, religion and landscape painting, and laid

The Alhambra in Granada, built in the fourteenth century, is an oasis in an arid location, divided into small and beautifully proportioned walled enclosures with pavilions, arched galleries and ingenious water features.

out according to strict rules. In the case of Japanese gardens, in particular, vegetation was often lacking – one of the most famous, the Ryoan-ji in Kyoto, which was constructed around 1500 AD, consists of carefully placed rocks surrounded by oceans of raked gravel – minimalism 500 years before it reached the West. This Eastern approach to gardens is one that has had particular resonance with architects and landscape designers of the twentieth century and up until the present day.

RENAISSANCE GARDENS

But swinging back to Europe, and to a time when gardens really started to make their mark, in order to understand a little about the development of Renaissance gardens in fifteenth century Italy, you need to have some idea of what the country was like in the centuries beforehand. For a start, Italy wasn't a country at all – it was a group of cities and provinces, all independent of each other, and often not particularly friendly either. The wealthy lived in castles they'd built for themselves, either out of reach on hilltops or hidden away behind high walls – with marauding gangs and rivals beyond the next valley, this was not the safest place in the world to be. And it seems shocking when you look back on it that much of the building material for those castles and roads and other works happening then was found under their feet in the form of ancient Roman remains, often already conveniently cut to size: what they considered old rubble came in handy.

Boccaccio wrote *The Decameron* in the fourteenth century, and this lusty tale, set in the countryside as a group of young people escape from the plague-ridden city, is essentially a call to leave the Dark Ages behind, a rallying

TOP: Japanese-American sculptor Isamu Noguchi's garden at his studio in Long Island City, now the Noguchi Museum, blends a Japanese aesthetic with modernism. Below: the influence of the garden design of Villa Lante reached far beyond Italy.

cry for Roman civilisation to rise once again. It coincided with increased trade around the Mediterranean; sailors came back with news of fantastic Moorish gardens in Spain, and Christians fleeing Constantinople brought knowledge to Italy of the ancient civilisation there. The time was ripe for a rebirth of an interest in arts and learning in this part of the world. This helped contribute towards a wonderfully classical style of architecture based on sound mathematical ratios and led to the garden being considered one place that combined mathematical principles with the arts in the most decadent way.

Florence was the centre to start with, and the Medici family had a crucial role in the development of arts, architecture and the garden. The family, who'd made their fortune in banking, had started off as unassuming peasant stock in the Tuscan countryside. Various family members became passionate sponsors of the arts and architecture and, as for gardens, it's thought by some that this interest derived from their rural background.

When you look at their greatest achievements, like the Boboli Gardens in Florence by Niccolò Pericoli (or il Tribolo, as he was known, a true Renaissance man, being a sculptor, architect and engineer) the idea of it being a reminder of their humble past seems far-fetched. Nature never looked as ordered and formal. In a time of peace, when castles no longer needed to be fortresses, the Boboli Gardens were created as a display of wealth and power, and as a symbol of man's dominance over the landscape. They came to be the model for many royal gardens around Europe, including Versailles. Marie de Medici, when she was Queen of France, asked architect Salomon de Brosse to reflect the spirit of the Boboli Gardens, which she remembered from childhood, in the design of the Luxembourg Gardens – this, you'd have to think, was much more the Medici style of nostalgia than any allusions to their peasant past.

The Boboli Gardens, like many others of the time, were based around a central axis, which begins in an amphitheatre behind the Pitti Palace and rises quickly up Boboli Hill, flanked by Romanesque statues, to a second amphitheatre encircling a large pond.

From this point, a borrowed vista of the Florentine landscape and city takes over the garden, but is, again, designed to reinforce the wealthy family's status to those below them.

A second axis runs from the top of the hill to another feature, the Fountain of Neptune. Intersected by terraces and meandering paths, this axis is surrounded by fountains and water features decorated with stalactites and other elaborate mouldings – constructing it was a nightmare as there was no water source available but, along with the other advances in arts and sciences at the time, innovations in engineering and technology made it all possible. Grottoes, fountains, sculptures, terraces and parterre gardens, which are a regular grid of small, symmetrical, often quite elaborate, gardens divided off from each other by low, clipped hedges, are all very distinctive features of Italian Renaissance gardens. So, too, are trees – mainly pine, oak and ilex – which partly replaced protective walls as the vertical element in the landscape.

Other Italian Renaissance gardens that had an enormous influence around Europe and even beyond include Villa Lante at Bagnaia and the highly exuberant Villa d'Este, which is not only regarded as the most important water garden in the world but also pays homage to classical antiquity, with its stone models of buildings and monuments of ancient Rome. Pirro Ligorio was involved in the design of both, even designing the actual villa of Villa d'Este and, in both, there's a strong geometric feel, with small symmetrical gardens arranged around a central axis. Along with its spectacular natural setting, the water aspect of Villa d'Este is a marvel – as well as numerous extravagant fountains, cascades and ponds, there is even a fully functioning water organ.

While the Italians were creating these marvels, the rest of Europe was looking on agog. At the time, the French were stuck in the mediaeval phase, with small kitchen gardens being just about all there was on the domestic front. It took Charles VIII to change that – when he came back from invading Italy at the end of the fifteenth century (claiming the Kingdom of Naples as his inheritance), part of his spoils included 22 Italian artists, one of whom was Pacello da Mercoliano, a Dominican friar, who had worked on Poggio Reale, a Neapolitan garden. Charles had ideas for the friar to create an Italianate wonder for him in France and, thus, you could say, the age of the celebrity gardener was born. If an Italian garden was a status symbol in Italy, then an Italian garden created by an Italian in France was almost too much. It was at Chateau d'Amboise, one of Charles's residences, that Pacello da Mercoliano laid out a formal Italianate garden, before later working at Blois.

However, it wasn't until the work of talented French gardener Jacques Mollet in the late 1500s at the Chateau d'Anet that the style was honed to become more as we know it today. Jacques still used a very Italianate style, but positioned the now noticeable parterres to be centred on the chateau. More importantly,

this work signalled the birth of a great gardening dynasty with Jacques using his work at the chateau to train his son, Claude, who developed the style further. Claude Mollet's own career far surpassed that of his father as he went on to become the premier gardener for three kings, Henri IV, Louis XIII and Louis XIV, with work that included Chateau de Fontainebleau and Chateau de Saint Germain. Claude's son, André, then used his father's established French style to gain commissions in Holland, Sweden and England.

It's unbelievable that the French style's reach across an entire continent was the result of one family, but the Mollet name has been linked with many of the great European gardens. Some of André's notable commissions abroad included work for Charles I in London, Queen Christina in Stockholm and works on St James Park during the English Restoration. In a strange coincidence, André's father, Claude, was also a godparent to the other great French landscape designer, André Le Nôtre, who is most well known for the Champs Elysées and the quintessential French garden at the palace of Versailles.

The great garden at Versailles is the pinnacle of what is regarded as baroque garden design. Built just after the French Renaissance and to designs penned by Le Nôtre, the garden became the biggest, most lavish and expansive construction in Europe. Backed by the egos of both Louis XIV and Le Nôtre, the garden was laid out on the southern side of the palace which, in itself, was the largest in the world, with the terrace surrounding the palace decoratively laid out in a parterre of buxus and annuals. The lower parts of the garden stretch as far as the eye can see, laid symmetrically around a central axis ending with the Grand Canal and the King's Forest. At the foot of the great staircase to the terrace is the Fountain of Latona, and towards the Grand Canal is the Fountain of Apollo – although the garden is a true French landscape, the use and extravagance of water can be easily traced back to its Italian heritage.

THE ENGLISH EXPERIENCE

The French architectural and cultural influence on England had been predominant for some years. Whether it was England's lack of cultural identity dragging on from feudalism or just that, as is still common in many places today, they were easily impressed by anything foreign, is hard to say but the French–Italian style dominated and influenced the design of all public parks and private landscapes from the early seventeenth century. But then a number of factors emerged to change that. Landscape art became popular; poets and writers such as Milton started writing about the beauty of nature; the Grand Tour became an essential part of life for British travellers, putting them into contact with nature at its wildest. English philosophy and thought, generally, seemed more elastic than that in France, and, on top of that, Lancelot 'Capability' Brown came along.

Brown wasn't the only designer of 'natural' landscapes by any means, but he's the most well-known and certainly the most radical. While those before him had tried to blend the formal with the informal, Brown was having none of that. From the 1740s onwards, he was ripping out quite beautiful and established structured gardens and replacing them with undulating parkland, clumps of trees and vast lakes. He wasn't interested in cultural references or symbolic structures – he received all his instructions from nature, and was aiming for grandiose simplicity and panoramic views rather than manmade wonders, providing a contrast to the classical domestic architecture that was popular at the time.

In many ways, Brown could be called the first of the 'fashionable' garden designers – he was incredibly popular in his day, but there was something almost wilful in his destruction of existing gardens. It's obviously not just a modern phenomenon to want to go with the latest trend, whether it's appropriate or not, or to have a lack of respect for anything that happens to be 'out of fashion'. But, one thing you can say for Brown is that he created the first truly English style of garden, and to create a staged natural setting with vistas and complex specimen plantings is more difficult than it looks. Many, though, have pointed out his shortsightedness, with renowned twentieth century English designer Russell Page being one of his harshest critics. 'Lancelot Brown was encouraging his wealthy clients to tear out their splendid formal gardens and replace them with his facile compositions of grass, tree clumps and rather shapeless pools and lakes.' It didn't stop the *jardin anglais* becoming a big hit in Europe – strangely enough, it was taken up particularly by the French and Italians, who were probably ready for a change from their more formal creations. The simple way French gardens are viewed may, in some ways, be their downfall. While a Landscape garden slowly reveals itself as one explores, a French parterre is often designed to be viewed from only one position. They may have features within them that warrant closer inspection but, providing your eyesight is good enough, that feature can often be seen from afar.

PREVIOUS PAGES: Villa d'Este, considered the most important water garden in the world, pays homage to classical antiquity. This page, top: elaborate parterre at Versailles. Below: at Longwood Gardens in Pennsylvania, water features, added in 1906, show definite European influences.

After Brown died in 1783, his place in garden history was taken by Humphry Repton, whose approach to design is one we still relate to today. Being more of a consultant than a garden contractor – producing plans and renderings rather than constructing gardens – he had far more commissions than any other English gardener. It's estimated that he designed more than 400 works. Not working in any one style, Repton received many commissions in which his role was to redesign or improve gardens installed by his predecessors. Formal gardens were framed with softer Picturesque landscape planting, while Landscape gardens were altered to provide decorative entertaining spaces or terraces, flower beds or fountains near the

open views of a nearby hillside or a church spire, to which the eye would be directed.

Thematic planning was also a feature of Repton's gardens, inspired by the landscapes and gardens of the Americas, Asia and Africa. Repton would create designs that were intended to amaze visitors with their display of the new and exotic. Creating an arboretum was one way of displaying the delights of a different continent or culture in a way that was easily assimilated into an English Picturesque garden style. The arboretum would contain trees collected on distant travels and provide a certain exotic ambience. This may well, in turn, have inspired the movement known as Gardenesque, a term first coined by garden designer and botanist John Loudon.

an artwork might be a focal point of a room today, a rare shrub from Indonesia, India or Africa may have taken pride of place in a Victorian garden. Loudon was a friend of Joseph Banks, the botanist and explorer, so perhaps it was hardly surprising that he was so interested in individual specimens. The plantings within the gardens also displayed a new approach to design. Large drifts replaced complex arrangements and thus a need for bigger, more textured or coloured foliage was required to keep things interesting. Drifts and shapes of both the plantings and the gardens themselves did, however, remain organic. Paths would meander around strategic plantings, to give you a chance to examine each carefully, and a straight line was a very rare occurrence.

Loudon, a fan of European formal gardens, was also on the brink of what we would call modern 'landscape architecture', with his first use of the term occurring when he referred to the Italianate Picturesque style garden at Deepdene, created by architect William Atkinson, as an example of landscape architecture. What Loudon liked about the idea was that the garden and house were considered together and made overall sense. In his 1833 *Encyclopaedia of Cottage, Farm and Villa Architecture*, he observed that in modern Italian villas, 'the regularity of the garden is, as it were, an accompanying decoration and support to the Architecture. The Architecture, sculpture and gardens of these villas are often designed by the same hand, and concur in the general effect to produce perfect harmony.' These days, the same hand doesn't apply itself to all aspects of the house and garden but, in a perfect world, all elements, too, should still be in 'perfect harmony'.

> Repton understood the idea of the borrowed vista, in which the surrounding landscape or architectural features can be claimed as part of the garden. This often meant the felling of stands of trees to create open views of a nearby hillside or a church spire.

house, something Brown would not have sanctioned at all. There was an understanding in Repton's designs, which gently led from the house into the surrounds, that the garden needed to have some kind of relationship with the architecture as well as provide a particular atmosphere, along with views, wherever possible. In Brown's world, the house was more of an irritation than anything else – views and the landscape were all that mattered.

Repton understood the idea of the borrowed vista, in which the surrounding landscape or architectural features can be claimed as part of the garden. This often meant the felling of stands of trees to create

The son of a farmer, Loudon's first experience was in the layout of agricultural lands, which quickly developed into a landscape design business and later into town planning. He was a prolific writer and between the 1820s and 1840s produced encyclopaedic books on plant types and design principles. The term Gardenesque first appeared in 1832, its main premise being that gardens should not be created as landscapes but be developed from carefully placed exotic specimens and abstract garden beds. This was a time of great exploration, and nothing was more prized than the latest new plant from some far-flung location. In the same way that

Loudon's influence was at a critical moment, when colonisation of the new world was a reality and it was becoming relatively easy to travel. That had two effects: more exotics became available in Europe, and design ideas quickly made their way to the colonies.

The interpretation of Gardenesque, combined with native flora and culture – exotic in themselves to the new residents – created many remarkable gardens. In America, Andrew Jackson Downing, garden writer and designer, was influenced by Loudon when creating, with Calvert Vaux, some of the United States' greatest landscapes, including the grounds of the Smithsonian Institute and the White House, both in Washington, DC. Downing was, himself, a great influence on landscape architect Frederick Law Olmsted who, after Downing's death, went on to create, with Vaux, one of the world's most enduring landscapes, New York's Central Park which, in the late 1850s, rose out of a swamp to become the first urban landscaped park in the United States. It was always Vaux and Olmsted's intention to have a bust of Downing in the park, but that never happened.

Australian garden design of the period also has much to thank Loudon for. The Governor's grounds in both Melbourne and Sydney are designed in typical Gardenesque mode, a style that is probably more suited to a warmer climate, allowing designers to use a far more interesting and exotic selection of species.

A BACKWARDS GLANCE

It wasn't until Gertrude Jekyll came on the scene in 1870 that things would change. She spearheaded the garden component of the Arts and Crafts movement and had the reputation of changing 'the face of England more than any save the Creator himself and, perhaps, Capability Brown'.

Jekyll, like Brown 150 years or so before her, reflected the tastes of the day. Interestingly, these thoughts weren't of the future but of a distant and idealised past. Prior to Jekyll's input, gardens had become more sophisticated. But then Jekyll and other members of the Arts and Crafts movement, including designer William Morris and architect Edward Lutyens, came along and set up a new way of looking at the world.

The Arts and Crafts movement was a product of its time. It came about partly as a reaction against industrialisation, which had had such a profound effect on everyone's lives, as well as on the quality of goods produced. Capitalism was born and, along with it, came a fear that the world was in a state of spiritual and moral decline, not to mention that artistic values were being lost as industrial production took over.

It was in this climate that the Arts and Crafts movement came about in the second half of the nineteenth century in Britain and slightly later in the United States and Australia. Its philosophies were based on a rejection of technological progress and a return to the handmade, with its influence spanning all forms of design from architecture and interior design to graphic design and landscaping. From its idealistic vision of small groups of artist-craftsmen working together came schemes that showed a remarkable sense of single-mindedness, from the design of the curtains and carpets to building materials used for the house and the layout of the garden.

The overall effect of the Arts and Crafts movement was as if the world was moving forward but someone was putting the brakes on, with the aim of trying to relive a romantic past. How this translated into gardens was a move away from the ordered and formal into something wilder, more self-sufficient and cottagey. Garden rooms needed to be stuffed with more perennials than they could cope with, the garden had to reflect the owner's personality and didn't take too much looking after, and, in an attempt not to look too contrived, a variety of materials were used.

The garden arm of the Arts and Crafts movement reached its peak with the collaboration between garden designer Gertrude Jekyll (who had trained as a painter) and architect Edward Lutyens. Rather than giving a strictly organic feel to the space, their designs were architectural in scope, each section being quite discrete, but always with completely spontaneous and colourful planting. Local materials were used as much as possible for pathways, steps and walls, and building methods were vernacular in character. Jekyll was famous for her herbaceous borders, which comprised the most extraordinary mix of common and grand plants – the rose with the sweet pea, the iris with the lupin. During her career, she designed more than 400 gardens, mainly for the nouveau riche, but also for more humble environments. If anything, Jekyll's most important contribution to gardening and design was the evolution of the backyard garden and the establishment of its cultivation as a popular pastime.

Jekyll's influence far exceeded that of her own creations, most of which no longer exist. It was her writing that had the greatest and longest lasting impact around the world – as well as producing 15 books, she also wrote more than 1000 articles for newspapers, journals and magazines.

Jekyll's counterpart in Australia was Edna Walling, as prolific a writer and photographer as she was a garden designer. She wrote four books, and had plans for many more, and contributed hundreds of articles to magazines and newspapers. Although influenced heavily by the works of Jekyll, Walling did have a particularly Australian slant to her romantic gardens, which included all the features you'd expect, like meandering pathways, stone walls, garden rooms and vegetable plots, and she was one of the first to recognise the beauty of native plants, becoming involved in the emerging conservation movement. As she wrote in her book *The Australian Roadside*: '…the continual scenes of unthinking devastation have made it difficult to remain quiet and it is hoped that in consequence of this book, some readers may not continue to view the roadside plants so much as "scrub" but as the very interesting, fitting and invaluable plants they really are'. And like the true exponents of the Arts and Crafts movement, Walling sought to create a sense of unity between house and garden, using the architecture as a starting point for the design of the garden, and making sure rooms, wherever possible, had a view of the garden in an attempt to blend indoors and outdoors. She also had a pragmatic approach, believing that maintenance should be kept to a minimum – while some of her gardens were for the wealthy, she also designed for the middle classes, who weren't over-endowed with either staff or time.

Jekyll's influence was also felt in the United States – Beatrix Farrand, a founder member of the American Society of Landscape Architects and one of the leading exponents of the Arts and Crafts style of gardens in that country, bought copies of Jekyll's planting plans and then set about also drawing up plans for all building work in her gardens, which required a higher degree of skill than her mentor possessed. One of her most well-known gardens was Dumbarton Oaks in Washington, DC, also made famous by a chamber concerto of the same name by Stravinsky.

AN EXOTIC INFLUENCE

A design movement that started in the United States at about the same time as the Arts and Crafts movement was developing in Britain was inspired by the Spanish missions built in the late eighteenth century in California. It was just as nostalgic as the Arts and Crafts movement, but more exotic, depending on an imported aesthetic rather than a historical one. While it had no impact in Europe, possibly because it was too close to home, the style became quite popular for domestic architecture in Australia, New Zealand and some of the Caribbean. In essence, the style of the Californian missions, often built around a courtyard and dependent upon a limited supply of building materials and an even more limited supply of skilled labour, included massive adobe walls, broad eaves, low sloping tile roofs, colonnaded walkways and terraced bell towers. Those original missions were modest and austere but by the time the style was adapted to domestic use and exported to the other side of the world, it ranged from the relatively unassuming to the positively elaborate. It turned into an amalgam of those eighteenth century Californian missions with either their genuine Spanish counterparts or, at the other extreme, the suburban bungalow – a case of the Antipodean Alhambra on one hand or, on the other, the three-bedroom, single-garage Alamo.

The exotic architecture cried out for an equally exotic garden – lupins, sweet peas and those other Arts and Crafts favourites wouldn't do. Instead, palms and succulents, aspidistra and clivia, orchids and hibiscus were an equal match for the far-from-indigenous style of design. And then there were essential elements in the garden – the water feature, the beautifully constructed brick pathways, often in the form of Moorish motifs, the terracotta pots of herbs or citrus fruits, the monastic sense of order underneath that exoticism. Like a number of periods of architecture and garden design over the ages, this was a time that saw the creation of contrived, stage-set environments – reality didn't come into play here, and there was nothing wrong with that.

And so while Spanish Mission was a contrast to Arts and Crafts, so too was a new style, Art Deco, which started at around the same time the Arts and Crafts movement was winding up. It's hard to imagine anything more different from the highly nostalgic Arts and Crafts – the only way Art Deco looked back was to rebel against the fussiness and excesses of Victorian and Edwardian design and head in the opposite direction, going for stylised decoration, a streamlined approach and a blend of the lavish and exotic with the more down to earth. Art Deco was happening at a time when there were great advances in materials and technology, which the movement embraced wholeheartedly. Some people date the start of Deco to 1925, the year of the Paris Expo, the Exposition Internationale des Arts Décoratifs et Industriels Modernes, while others think it started at least 10 years before that. Exactly what constitutes Art Deco is also open to debate but, basically, as far as domestic architecture goes, a typical Deco house is

THE START OF THE MODERN

How Art Deco architecture related to its surrounds is quite different from the Arts and Crafts concept of house and garden merging into one romantic whole. Garden designers were flummoxed by Art Deco – the modernity and starkness of the house didn't seem to warrant a garden. The high tech architecture didn't work as a starting point for developing a landscaping scheme – no wonder many designers decided to leave the house, in all its austere beauty, in a similarly plain landscape, with perhaps little more than a built-in window box to display signs of life. The leap from nostalgia to a futuristic slant would need time to develop, although Gabriel Guevrekian's garden at the 1925 Paris Expo, described by the UK Department of Trade as 'more ingenious than beautiful' was ahead of its time, with a wall of triangles of green and red glass, triangular lawns and tilted triangular beds of begonias, a triangular fountain with rotating sphere on top, and lighting for night-time drama. Patron of the arts Charles de Noailles was more impressed by it than the Trade Department, as he commissioned Guevrekian to design him an abstract triangular cloister-like garden (derided by contemporary critics as 'curious and sinister') for his modern house at Hyères in the South of France.

Art Deco moves seamlessly into the Modernist movement – the Deco curves might have disappeared but, otherwise, the love of the unadorned, of technology and of modern materials is constant, and the approach to the garden is remarkably similar between the two.

TOP: the garden at Hatfield House in Hertfordshire was laid out in the early seventeenth century, using plants, trees and bulbs brought in from Europe, and never before seen in England. Below: Capability Brown was commissioned to transform the gardens at Chatsworth in Derbyshire.

The garden at Little Sparta in Scotland was created by true Renaissance man Ian Hamilton Finlay as a beguilingly romantic blend of horticulture and sculpture. Throughout the garden are his installations, often bearing inscriptions spelling out his witty take on the world.

One architect who stands alone at this time is Frank Lloyd Wright, who worked in the United States for the first half of the twentieth century. Although his designs were uncompromisingly modern in some respects, much of their influence came from the land on which they were built. His most famous, Falling Water, a house built near Pittsburgh in the Thirties, is revolutionary – the cantilevered, terraced structure seems to grow out of the land with, as its name suggests, a stream and waterfall flowing under the building itself.

Wright's sensitivity is summed up in his writings on the siting of his own house: '…this place now called Taliesin is built like a brow on the edge of the hill – not on top of the hill – because I believe you should never build on top of anything directly. If you build on top of the hill, you lose the hill.'

Wright was influential around the world, and so too, but in an entirely different way, was Swiss-born architect Le Corbusier, whose seriously modern buildings from the Twenties continue to inspire. It wasn't just the buildings that he was interested in, though; he was one of the first to get a real handle on what a modern garden could be. Some of his works, including the Villa Savoie outside Paris and the Unité d'Habitation in Marseille, have roof terraces, which are as much pieces of sculpture as they are gardens, and draw from classical principles of composition and basic geometric forms in their design and construction. The same approach was also taken by the Bauhaus school in Germany, which was set up by Walter Gropius in 1919 with the aim of integrating various strands of art, design, architecture, economics and engineering into a democratic and streamlined whole. While gardens didn't figure highly on their list of priorities, when they did, their design, featuring neat slabs of grass, paving and ordered planting, matched the geometry of the buildings themselves.

Some of those Bauhaus designers left Europe and moved to the United States, Australia and other parts of the world before or during the Second World War, taking their principles with them, and influencing generations who came into contact with their work. After the war, the wealth in the United States was almost unimaginable – combine that with the artistic and architectural talent and thought around at the time, and the results were staggering. Architects and landscape designers worked together to create integrated indoor and outdoor spaces. Harvard-educated Dan Kiley, for instance, worked with architect Eero Saarinen on the Miller house and garden in Indiana, inspired by Mies van der Rohe's Barcelona Pavilion and the De Stijl movement, and presenting a flow from grid-planned garden to meadow to woods – a blend of modernist ideas and traditional principles. On a slightly different note, one of the most exceptional modernist gardens in the United States is by sculptor Isamu Noguchi in the grounds of his warehouse studio in Long Island City, now open to visitors as the Noguchi Museum.

Roberto Burle Marx, a Brazilian landscape designer, studied fine arts in Germany before returning to Brazil, where he also hooked up with a number of architects, including Oscar Niemeyer, who had been influenced by Le Corbusier. The most notable feature of Burle Marx's approach to landscape design from the Thirties onwards was in his use of native plants, an idea that has since been picked up by designers all over the world. It fits in with modernist principles, being functional, in a sense, and applying an honest use of materials. Seeing nurseries these days packed with natives, it's hard to believe that in many places, including Australia, they were virtually impossible to get hold of a few decades ago.

When you come across a place like Little Sparta, in the Pentland Hills in Scotland, there's reason to believe poetry still exists in the garden.

That use of natives has managed to, at least partly, instil some degree of local content and context into gardens that, during the height of modernism, became so globalist and abstract as to be almost meaningless.

It's hard to say what will happen after the coolness of modernism in the garden, which is still relevant to the minimalist lines of many houses built today. But when you come across Little Sparta in the Pentland Hills in Scotland, started in 1966 by Ian Hamilton Finlay, there's reason to believe poetry still exists in the garden. A fusion of horticulture and sculpture, it is home to his simple installations, which appear in glades and on pathways, and range from obelisks and benches to plaques and bridges. Created in collaboration with stonemasons and letter-cutters, they spell out in stone, wood and metal his philosophy and gently witty take on the world. 'Certain gardens are described as retreats when they really are attacks,' he once said. It's true that here you discover that nothing really new exists in the garden – the past, we see so often, provides the bedrock for the present, and a constant source of inspiration and nourishment for the future.

Renaissance Gardens

Straight lines, symmetry, an interesting arrangement of plants and attention to detail are all features of the true Renaissance garden.

THE RENAISSANCE OF the fifteenth century was, as its name suggests, a rebirth, a reworking of all areas of culture and thought. It was seen in the art and writing of the period, in science, mathematics and philosophy and, in fact, all areas of human endeavour. That included the garden which, in previous times in Europe, almost always had a practical purpose, whether that be as a place to grow medicinal herbs or as a small and temporary retreat from the challenges of the outside world. During the Renaissance, which started in Italy, particularly in Florence, before spreading to France, the garden shook off that practical mantle and became an artwork in itself, designed using newly discovered mathematical principles and reflecting the philosophies of the time. Not only did it function as a living artwork but the garden was also seen as a symbol of wealth and power, created as much to impress as for personal enjoyment.

The power wasn't only directed towards those who stood in awe of the garden but also towards the land itself – Renaissance gardens, typically, were not limited by landforms but tried to express dominance over them. Starting with a clean slate and not influenced in the least by topography or existing vegetation, designers, with access to the most brilliant engineers of the time, created their ideal gardens, which were formal and stylistic in design. House and garden were designed as one, and how that translates to re-creating a Renaissance garden today is that the house is often used as a starting point for the garden, with axes drawn from a particular detail – the roofline, the physical centre of the building or some other architectural feature.

Straight lines and symmetry are essential elements of a Renaissance garden, forming the basis around which to work. The key is to be quite linear in your approach, using a long axis as the framework, with garden 'rooms' formed off that. The main difference between the Renaissance garden and its later counterparts is in the type of plants used. The Renaissance garden consists of very few plants, and those that are used are usually in the form of hedging which, as part of its function, separates one garden room from another. Detail is found in the craft of hedging, which can include very elaborate parterres, rather than in the interesting arrangement of plant types; it's a demonstration of horticultural skills rather than, as was later the case, the owner's adventures around the world. Colour in the Renaissance garden comes in the form of occasional annuals or strategically placed urns of flowers, but these should be used judicially and not overdone.

Buxus and yew were common hedging plants in those times, and still are today. Escallonia is another possibility. In the past, gardeners and owners had to wait for years for the garden to grow – now, when we're used to instant gratification in all aspects of our lives and are not prepared to wait for anything, it's possible to buy, admittedly at a price, a 4-metre-high (12-foot-high) clipped plane tree hedge in order to create a garden immediately. You may think that takes away some of the enjoyment and satisfaction of gardening but, these days, patience isn't necessarily regarded as a virtue.

The grander Renaissance gardens were a reconstruction of the world, often dissolving into nearby woodland and including staged spaces for hunting, not something you'd find in many modern reinterpretations. What you do find, though, is often a walled area close to the house used as a kitchen garden, planted with vegetables, herbs and often roses or other flowering plants.

Of course, we live entirely different lives from members of the aristocracy of the fifteenth and sixteenth centuries, and our gardens should reflect that. Re-creating in purist form a Renaissance garden, or any other garden, for that matter, doesn't make sense – it should be adapted and reinterpreted to suit today's lifestyles, but taking inspiration from the original. Nowadays we use the outdoors more than ever before – it's hard to picture the Medici family, for instance, having an alfresco lunch, whereas it's impossible to imagine not using the garden that way now. And so, even in a seemingly authentic 'modern' Renaissance garden, you'd almost certainly want to incorporate an outdoor entertaining space. This would probably be placed close to the house for easy access, but can, like other elements of the garden, be created by following those same mathematical principles, siting the area on an axis line and perhaps bordering it with a low hedge to form another garden room. Approached skilfully, the space wouldn't look even slightly out of place in a genuine Renaissance setting.

View of the formal landscaping below the belvedere in the garden at La Foce in Tuscany. Areas have been divided off using buxus, a hedging plant that was as commonly used in Renaissance times as it is today.

LA FOCE

Val d'Orcia, Tuscany

I FIRST FOUND out about the garden at La Foce from Matt and Clare Handbury, the current tenants of Bronte House, who came by the garden during an Italian holiday. Clare had bought the beautiful book *La Foce: A Garden and Landscape in Tuscany* and, knowing my passion for garden books and design, let me borrow it for a weekend. The pictures and description of the property by Morna Livingston and Benedetta Origo made me want to visit the garden the next day. One of the few disadvantages of living in Australia is that the rest of the world is very far away. Despite my longing, it was not until I had the excuse of a trip to the Chelsea Flower Show that I would get a chance to visit the garden.

My plan was simple: go to Chelsea, rendezvous with my better half, Kate, in Paris for a long-awaited overseas holiday, head down to the south of France, pop across to Italy and happen to stop by La Foce on the way to Rome. The perfect trip, I thought to myself, and everything was moving along swimmingly until I realised that La Foce is only open to visitors on Wednesdays, and my holiday arrangements had me leaving Florence on Thursday. Half a world away and I would miss out on visiting my dream destination. And this would certainly have been the case had it not been for the grace of the garden's owner, Benedetta Origo.

La Foce is the name of the large estate that lies within the Val d'Orcia (Orcia Valley), located between the towns of Pienza, Montepulciano and Chianciano Terme. It once consisted of a mediaeval castle, Castelluccio (little castle), and 57 farm buildings on 3190 hectares (7882 acres) of farmlands and woods, elements of which date back many thousands of years. It's a spectacular part of the Tuscan countryside, but one that has only become so because of the dedication of the farmers and the Origo family.

Bought in 1924 by Antonio and Iris Origo, La Foce existed under a co-op arrangement. Farmers of Val d'Orcia would create produce for La Foce, the sale of which would fund the community and household. At the time they took it over, however, Antonio and Iris had inherited an unprofitable wasteland with no community infrastructure and buildings falling into disrepair. Through hard work and an understanding of the environment, the valley was transformed into what is now commonly regarded as the pride of the Tuscan countryside.

The building the Origos decided to make their family home was actually the home of the then property overseer. The previous owners of the property had lived in the more significant Castelluccio, which the Origos decided to reserve for community use.

The house at La Foce dates back to the fifteenth century, when the villa was used as an inn, said to be a popular resting spot for travellers on the route to and from Rome. The property, however, has an even longer history as the Castelluccio, located on a nearby hill, is believed to have been built in the eleventh century and, preceding that, the land was once an Etruscan settlement dating back to the seventh century BC. As an Australian, it's almost impossible to fathom such age, as permanent building work did not occur until the British arrived in the eighteenth century, and it's rare to come across a property older than 150 years.

After buying their new home, Antonio and Iris employed the services of English architect Cecil Pinsent. Iris already knew Cecil as he had worked on her mother's house, Villa Medici, in Fiesole, and the nearby house of friend Bernard Berenson, Villa I Tatti. On these two properties Cecil had proved not only that he could design and redesign a home, but also that he was also talented in creating landscapes.

The entry to La Foce is a wonderfully understated yet opulent setting. Serious gates meet you at the street but behind them is a wonderful array of complex garden beds planted with echium and buxus and a short avenue of pencil pines. You feel as though you have entered straight into the garden rather than into an imposing drive and forecourt – it's intimate and welcoming, and there's nothing intimidating or pretentious about it. The house itself is blocked from the drive, and entry is via a pair of topiary evergreen oaks, *Quercus ilex*.

A view from the lemon garden of the inner courtyard, situated in front of the *salone*. Along the central axis of the design stands a pond, in the middle of which is an antique fountain decorated with stone dolphins.

Early photos of the entry show that the left hand oak had some age to it when the garden was being developed, while the one on the right was a mere sapling. Although the garden has been in place now for the best part of 80 years, I still find it amazing that both trees now look exactly the same.

The trees now screen much of the front of the villa, and although this would be a travesty on a grand house, it isn't of concern to La Foce, partly because the villa was once an inn, later a farmer's house, and from the street that's what it remains. There's something very honest about that street façade and I'm glad they haven't tried to change it. I like the rendered walls and red brick trim; it's very rural and in

The overall feeling in the garden at La Foce is of the Renaissance. A central axis can be drawn from the south-west facing rear wing rooms, past the inner garden and fountain, through a box parterre and beyond to Pinsent's final works, an extraordinary grotto pond and grand travertine steps. Cross axes form intermittent vistas through this line and also provide the garden with greater depth. It is often forgotten that the Italians invented the symmetrical landscape style and the parterre. At La Foce, the geometric nature of the house lends itself to the creation of these spaces, but it is the landscape that provides the setting for the varied array of garden rooms.

Pinsent was on the edge of Arts and Crafts, but rather than sticking to this style, his design is successful as an amalgamation of period styles.

keeping with the area. The greater part of the house behind it, though, is somewhat different.

Pinsent's work opened up the rooms in the house; he provided light to the darker areas through the use of skylights and fitted it out with an eclectic mix of eighteenth century multicultural styling. As well as decorating the interior, he also constructed a garage and several outbuildings, and extended the *fattoria* to form a courtyard, which is a real feature of the house. His work on La Foce was not finished until 1939, 15 years after he started.

More important now than the villa at La Foce is the garden, probably Pinsent's greatest work as a quasi-garden designer. Pinsent was on the edge of my least favourite garden style, Arts and Crafts, but rather than sticking to this style, his design is successful as an amalgamation of period styles suited to the given architecture.

The inner courtyard and lower garden outside the *salone* were the first to be designed and built. The lower court forms an external foyer for visitors. It is simple, with lemons in terracotta pots mounted on plinths in a bare lawn, with the odd perennial providing colour throughout the year. The inner courtyard is a little more 'gardeny' and, as the main feature directly off the house, it needs to be. In the centre is a pond with an antique fountain of stone dolphins. This is in line with the central axis of the design, and guests are forced to walk around the space via garden beds filled with lavender, tulips and clipped buxus. A clever grotto made from plumbago looks towards the centre of the garden and provides the first of many resting and reflecting spots. Iris Origo once told a friend that what she wanted was a garden 'in which to read and think'. In this garden she had that opportunity.

THIS PAGE: the lemon garden, which also acts as an external foyer for visitors. Fairly simple in design, it consists of lemons in terracotta pots mounted on plinths on the lawn, with the occasional perennial to provide colour. Following pages: the *limonaia*, the winter retreat for the potted citrus.

The *limonaia* is one of my
favourite buildings at La Foce,
and the design of the adjacent
pool is perfectly suited to it.

Six years after the first garden construction, Pinsent extended the landscape further out along his new axis to create a formal parterre in which potted lemons could be kept throughout the warmer months. Unlike most parterres, this garden is an array of different heights. Clipped domes in the buxus create a strong architectural feel, and although it is a very carefully clipped space it is equally kept horticulturally biased by the presence of manicured weeds. Campanula drips from cracks in the stonework, wisteria rambles over the surrounding walls and pink geraniums spring up from every other free space. Pomegranates provide some seasonal interest on the wall separating this lemon garden from the inner garden, and peonies provide huge bursts of pink in the right season.

Before I visited La Foce, I didn't realise how successful campanula could be as a massed plant. Rather than keeping it low to the ground where it usually belongs, it has been elevated and can be appreciated in the same way as a picture hung on a wall. It is particularly good behind the wisteria-covered arbour in the lemon garden, highlighting a shady spot that would normally be quite dull.

At the end of the axis is one of the most extravagant installations in a private garden I have seen. Pinsent's final extension to the garden was the installation of a set of travertine steps from a belvedere which enclosed a grotto. The belvedere provides a full stop to the axis from the house, and commands a view of the surrounding Val d'Orcia. One feature in the view, a twisting road on the hill opposite the villa, has become synonymous with Tuscany itself. The road was built in 1935 by the Origos and valley workers as a utilitarian construction during the establishment of their agricultural

TOP: a view of the lemon garden, showing the immaculately clipped buxus hedging. Below: the inner courtyard garden, directly off the house, has beds filled with lavender and tulips with buxus surrounds. Following pages: the belvedere has commanding views over Val d'Orcia.

CLOCKWISE FROM TOP LEFT: classical statues are very much part of a Renaissance garden; a view from the belvedere across to the zigzag road, which has become synonymous with the Tuscan countryside but was built only in 1935 by the Origos; bench in the courtyard garden near the house.

endeavours, and as a symbol of achievement for the farmers, but surely there was some aesthetic foresight behind its creation.

The grotto under the belvedere is of travertine, and contains a stunning three-tier fountain. Both Pinsent and Iris loved the rough look of the stone, which has been used in paths, walls and for furniture. In front of the grotto is a formal box parterre of arrowhead design. The lowest part of the axis of the garden is focused around a travertine pond and bench flanked by conifers. Pinsent designed all the garden's furniture and, although it is a bit ornate for my liking, it resides perfectly in the location.

Adjacent to the great formal garden is a long rose and wisteria arbour. Its structure provides much needed height as well as a leafy backdrop to the low formal lemon garden. The arbour eventually leads to a grape pergola

of pinks and blues in the form of iris, peonies and foxgloves.

The upper half of the garden is more of an eclectic arrangement of specimen trees and rows of old fruit trees, arranged over a terraced hillside. Two paths with steps built into the hill provide a track to climb to the top and on to moorland. From up there, the outlook is stunning, with one path lined with tall trees framing the view to a distant ancient military tower in the centre of Val d'Orcia, while the other catches a keyhole view of the Origos' famous zigzag road.

The original road, via Francigena, ran right past the front door of what was then the inn, and beyond what is now the *limonaia*, lawn and pool. The new design by Pinsent took into account that access to the surrounding landscape needed to be maintained, but added a sense of grandeur

an entertaining space. A single stone bench is the only form of ornamentation in the *limonaia* lawn, which I find a refreshing change.

Today, under the management of Antonio and Iris's daughters, Benedetta and Donata, La Foce has had somewhat of a renaissance itself, moving away from farming and into the business of tourism. This has led to a flurry of restoration and renovation which, of course, has been carried out in a beautiful and skilfully understated way.

One of the truisms of design is that when you do something right, no one will notice, but when something is done poorly, everyone will see it. In the garden, Pinsent's design has been maintained, and new plantings continue to be added. Saplings at the end of the long grape arbour will eventually form an arboretum that will seamlessly blend into the surrounding woodland, and the perennial plantings have a simple, timeless appearance. Inspired by the original garden, and with an Origo sense of style, the surrounding residences, fitted out as holiday houses, are also receiving gardens and landscapes of their own, admittedly none as grand as the villa's but suited to their own stature in the landscape.

The garden at La Foce is a testament to great design. The landscape works; it feels Italian and as if it belongs to a fifteenth-century house.

and the edge of an arboretum and meadow, changing the overall feel to a rather English or Landscape-inspired garden.

From this long walk it is possible to access the very Arts and Crafts rose garden. In here, hybrid teas are arranged in colours, and lavender separates the garden from the wisteria on the arbour. Not so strangely, though, my favourite rose in the garden is the 'Pierre de Ronsard', a rose I try to use on any job that requires a climbing flowering plant. Typically at La Foce, it grows like a weed, springing up from a gap in a travertine retaining wall near the belvedere. The rose garden also contains a very English perennial garden largely made up

and formality to La Foce by creating a driveway to the house that would be framed and reinforced by a series of outer walls and intersecting vistas. Making an entry in the outer forecourt, outside the gates, allowed everything inside the property to be dedicated to the garden.

The *limonaia* is one of my favourite La Foce buildings. Held within a conifer-bound lawn, it is approximately 30 metres long and 5 metres wide (100 feet by 15 feet) and, as its name suggests, is the winter retreat for the garden's potted citrus. The adjacent pool is perfectly suited to the building which, provided it's not full of lemons, can be used as

The garden of La Foce is a testament to great design. Although influences are apparent from the English and Arts and Crafts movements, the landscape works. It feels Italian; it feels as if it truly belongs to a fifteenth-century house. Iris Origo became well known for writing about subjects ranging from Byron's daughter to life in the Italian countryside under Mussolini. But while the texts, although admired, remain static, it is wonderful to see that her garden and landscape will continue to grow and develop and live on.

PARTERRE

Like an elaborate Persian rug, a parterre is the culmination of many years of development, in which plants have replaced wool, and a gardener the weaver. Parterres, which originated in France and Italy, became popular all over Europe, with two of the greatest being at Het Loo in the Netherlands, and at the palace of Versailles in France. Parterres, like the one at La Foce, shown here, use intricate buxus patterning combined with lawn and occasional gravel fillers, which provide either coloured or muted backgrounds.

HYDROLOGY

The founders of modern gardening, the Italians were masters of all landscaping elements, developing an understanding of horticulture, design and engineering. For the Italians, the use of water in the garden was the epitome of good design, but with their talents, it would be more of a theatrical showpiece than the serene vista we've come to expect from water features. The fountains and cascades at Villa Lante, shown here, are some of the first and best the Italians ever constructed and the inspiration for future designs around Europe.

HEDGES

Buxus or box is one of the most versatile plants in the world of garden design. It can be a gentle plant left to its own natural ways, or can be clipped into clouding shapes. Box is the most common plant used in topiary, its basic shape responding well to being sculpted into all sorts of exotic forms. As well, it can form part of the garden's structure, as it has at La Foce. The clipped buxus used throughout is as important structurally to the garden as the steps, paths and walls, its position in the landscape creating the basis for the garden's layout.

in detail

RENAISSANCE GARDENS

GRAND VIEW

The view from the palace at Versailles is one of the most spectacular vistas of all time. As a horticulturalist, it's hard not to think about all the work that's gone into clipping the hedges, but as a designer, you have to admire Le Nôtre's statement of power, which is in a class of its own, never to be repeated. To give some idea of the scale of the garden, it takes four hours to walk from the palace to the end of the Great Lake and back. Intersecting vistas, a replica English town and many roundels will distract you, but it is a worthy achievement.

GERANIUMS

The scented geranium, in an urn on top of the belvedere at La Foce, is a very Italianate feature in itself. Renaissance gardens are green gardens and it's only by the use of potted plants and some annuals that you get any seasonal interest; otherwise, the garden looks the same all year round. Geraniums are perfectly suited to the Mediterranean climate – they love a dry, sunny position and well-drained soil, which is exactly what they have in this garden. The pots are terracotta, which is porous, and, when I checked the potting mix, I found it was quite gravelly, which is similar to the type of soil in the garden.

STONE

All the structural garden paths and features in the garden at La Foce have been created from travertine marble, a material with a rustic quality that instantly provides a feeling of age, without losing the definition of the structure. When owner Iris Origo and architect Cecil Pinsent first laid the capping stone for their structures, they would have had immediate gratification from the appearance of their creations – the quirks and non-uniform texture of the stone would have looked tooled or weathered before even one day in the wind and rain.

Jacobean
(Landscape) Gardens

Working as it does with the landscape, highlighting natural elements and celebrating plants and trees in their unadorned state, there's something quite modern about the Landscape garden.

EIGHTEENTH CENTURY ENGLAND might seem a strange time and place to be talking about the birth of fashion and trends but, in some ways, there are enormous similarities between then and now. I've always loved the quote from British gardening designer Russell Page, referring to Lancelot 'Capability' Brown as the great destroyer of gardens, and I couldn't agree more. Capability Brown had his ideas, and nothing was going to get in his way – if that meant getting rid of a beautifully structured garden that had been there for 50 years but didn't fit with his way of thinking, that was fine. We can look back in horror now at all the gardens he must have ruined but it's easy to imagine his point of view – those gardens weren't particularly old at the time, just old fashioned; they hadn't been there long enough to warrant any special treatment. That line of thinking is so similar to that of today – something from a few seasons ago looks out of date to us and we can't see its merits, but give it several decades and we want to start looking after it, saving it and restoring it.

To Capability Brown there was no happy medium between the 'old fashioned' structured gardens and the Landscape gardens he was proposing – he couldn't see any benefit of structured areas around the house, for instance, and couldn't wait to get rid of them. It's that kind of dogmatic approach that continues today in the creation of so-called fashionable gardens, which are often quite inappropriate for their settings. Depending on what they contain – blue and white plants, certain type of grasses, for instance, or whatever else happens to be popular at the time – it's often possible to put an exact year on particular gardens, and that's not to be encouraged. The one thing you can say for Brown is that, for the first time in history, he designed truly English gardens – nothing was copied from Europe.

Unsurprisingly, the Landscape approach lends itself to larger scale gardens and in a time when global warming and water shortages have become part of our everyday concerns, environmentally, it's one of the better approaches to take.

At its best, the Landscape garden works with the contours of the land – there's no need to flatten out the entire countryside, as would be the case with some of the earlier types of garden. The idea is to work with what you've got, which may mean existing structured areas of the garden and other features, and that's fine – Capability Brown may not have approved, but that sense of evolution of a garden can be one of its most attractive features.

As well, it's important for the structure of the house to continue into the landscaping – while, again, Brown may not have thought it was important to tie the two together, we live differently today and the indoor/outdoor lifestyle is more or less taken for granted.

The Landscape garden lends itself perfectly to the formation of arboreta, which give the gardener an opportunity to develop horticulturally. The idea is to build up various collections of trees, and it's entirely up to you whether they're endemic or exotic. Depending on where you are, you could create a grove of peppermint gum or scribbly gum which, I know from gardens I've seen, can look quite brilliant or, in Europe, perhaps quercus or something from the betulus, or beech, family. Whatever you choose, it has to be in keeping with the natural surroundings, and one of the joys, in a sense, of creating a Landscape garden is in gaining an awareness of the natural environment, and understanding its strengths and limitations.

In setting up your collection of trees, the beauty is in the grove itself rather than in the way those individual trees are maintained, and this makes it quite different from a Renaissance garden. There's something outdated in the amount of effort a Renaissance garden takes to maintain – the number of man hours, not to mention carbon dollars, that go into creating hedging and other stylised features is too much for most people to justify. In that sense, there's something quite modern about a Landscape garden – it doesn't take an extraordinary amount of maintenance and, with its relatively simplified and natural scheme, can often be the perfect backdrop for a modernist style of architecture.

In a Landscape garden, the setting itself is paramount, and is celebrated in its own right. Natural features such as a rockery or even a cliff face can be highlighted or incorporated into the overall scheme. While roads and pathways meandering through the landscape have a definite and quite obvious function, they can also be used to lead the eye to the various features of the garden, which all combine to create nature at its manmade best.

The wonderfully simple estate fencing enclosing a paddock at Stourhead, considered the best 'Brownian landscape never to be touched by Brown'. The landscape at Stourhead benefits from being in an area of great natural beauty.

The original building on the property was demolished in the early eighteenth century by Henry Hoare I, who replaced it with Stourhead, perhaps Britain's most spectacular Palladian-style house. Work on the garden started about 20 years later.

STOURHEAD

Stourton, Warminster, Wiltshire

STOURHEAD, AN ORIGINAL landscape of the eighteenth century, doesn't seem fitting for a book on new gardens created around older architecture, but I'm including it because it's been so important to my work. It has served both as an inspiration for many of my larger works, and as a lesson in historic garden management and design.

The garden has been referred to as the best 'Brownian landscape never to be touched by Brown', and I like that quote. It challenges trends, and places doubt on a movement and design style generally regarded as gospel.

Stourhead, despite being a gigantic Landscape garden, is usable. It contains the most picturesque vistas, and held within its arboreta is one of the greatest arrays of plant materials of any English garden. It is even more of a complete garden than any of Brown's. The mixed foliage of the many trees provides a forever changing backdrop to the garden's many features, and the placement of the trees forces your eye to view the landscape only as its creator wanted you to. It's a garden that also evokes emotion, something I don't usually get in the broad turfed expanses of a Brown landscape.

The vast landscape was created by Henry Hoare II, grandson of Hoare's Bank founder, Sir Richard Hoare. Henry's father, Henry Hoare I, had bought the property in 1717 from Sir John Stourton and demolished the original house, Stourton Manor, to replace it with Stourhead, a spectacular house built in the popular Palladian style. The garden was, however, not developed until the 1740s, when Henry II took over the family estate after the death of his parents.

Created away from the house in a valley at the head of the River Stour, Stourhead is a landscape blessed with extraordinary natural beauty. The key to its design is a lake which forms its central hub and provides contrast and distant views. Too picturesque and perfect to be true, the great lake is actually manmade, its creation almost certainly inspired by works of art of the time depicting utopian gardens. The design and style of the garden is unique, rejecting the then popular baroque French landscape of symmetry, long avenues and parterres.

When I was researching the garden's inspiration, I thumbed through the works of Gaspard Dughet, a French artist who spent much of his time painting idealist scenery around Rome. Looking at these paintings, it is easy to see why Henry Hoare would want to emulate such visions of paradise. Even his fascination with architecture can be seen as an example of life imitating art.

Much of the garden at Stourhead is about creating a picture-perfect view or setting. As you walk from the house to the garden proper, keyhole vistas are presented to you. The first is a glimpse of the Temple of Apollo, which appears unexpectedly and much larger than you imagine. Further views are seen from the walk which meanders around the great lake and shoots off to the varying garden follies, from grottoes and Palladian bridges to the monolithic Pantheon.

I have been fortunate in my short time as a landscape designer to have worked on a surprisingly large number of large-scale gardens. My time at Sydney's Botanic Gardens reminds me of the Stourhead setting, with the great lake replaced by the harbour (you'll need to use your imagination). Set in a shallow valley, one country garden I'm involved in will, I hope, one day come to fruition as a Stourhead down under.

Working with an inspired property owner, my own landscape garden design uses the principles set by Henry II nearly 300 years ago and half a world away. Vistas have been narrowed or expanded upon, lakes and architecture draw the eye, and a mixed arboretum of over 600 native eucalypts and exotic species laid out in drifts, specimens and roundels provide the setting.

Unlike Henry, I have created the garden from bulldozer and laser level, which included constructing close to 250 metres (225 yards) of dry stone walls. The lakes were carved out in days and the garden is watered by a complex array of catchments, pipes and pumps. The greater landscape is close to 12 hectares (30 acres) and, as today's standards go, it's a big garden, with all the elements of construction bigger than anything I had ever created before. The unfortunate truth is that this soon-to-be magnificent garden is, most likely, a once-in-a-lifetime creation. Gardens like this take time, vision and obviously a great deal of money. Shrinking spaces, smaller budgets, increasing rules and regulations are facts of life in the modern world.

In my opinion, Stourhead as a modern garden would never exist. There isn't a council in the world that would let a gardener dam a valley for aesthetics; the labour required to develop the stunning Palladian structures would be too expensive, and the concept would be shunned by the design constabulary as egotistical and irresponsible. But the simple fact that this great garden exists – that a private garden has been created to this size and stature – makes it a special place.

In 1946, Henry Hugh Arthur Hoare gave Stourhead to the National Trust, the organisation set up for the preservation of culturally important structures and landscapes in England, Wales and Northern Ireland. Henry had restored much of the garden and the house over his own years at the property, but saw that the longevity of the home would only be achievable through opening the property to the public and under the guiding hand of an organisation with the infrastructure to support it.

The National Trust has done a wonderful job with the garden at Stourhead. An institutionalised private garden is a fairly new idea, and one often associated with the demise of the landscape. The property becomes the responsibility of often slow-moving committees and historians more concerned with how the garden existed than with how it can move forward.

A client of mine, who has a very good understanding of gardens, architecture and design, once referred to these types of historians as necrophiliacs, lovers of the dead and dusted. A gardener should always look to tomorrow, as a static garden is a dead garden, and understanding the past does not mean we should live in it.

In 1978, a plan of long-term management of the Stourhead garden was formulated and written up, supporting its development rather than letting it die – as, unfortunately, a number of heritage gardens do – a slow painful death of 'historian-itis'.

The plan was simple: where Henry Hoare II's designs have survived, they should be respected; 'replanting should follow precedent'; the garden should merge seamlessly with the wider landscape; and 'replanting should aim at simplicity rather than striking variety of colour and shape'.

It is a safe approach and one that I have used successfully, albeit a little bit more flamboyantly, on designs based around Victorian landscapes.

When I visited Stourhead for the first time, I entered via the gatehouse and garden entry adjacent to the house. Lining the driveway are 400-year-old oak trees, many of which are hollow and now only exist because of their cambium and a mountain of scar tissue.

Because of the sheer size of the Palladian structure, I found the house to be very enclosed by the drive, and difficult to appreciate without entering the adjacent paddock, which is bordered by estate fencing.

At the time of my visit, I happened to be designing a concept for a new garden for Leo Schofield, with whom I'd worked at Bronte House (page 104). His new house in Tasmania was a stunning Georgian manor and he gave me instructions to note any estate fencing details I found interesting, and so Stourhead became part of the research for the Tasmanian garden. Incidentally, the paddock at Stourhead has a small but beautiful kissing gate.

Obviously I'd seen photos of Stourhead, but one thing that surprised me when I got there was the distance between the garden and

Stourhead as a modern garden would never exist. No council in the world would let a gardener dam a valley for aesthetics; the labour required to develop the Palladian structures would be too expensive, and the concept would be shunned as egotistical.

the house. It had always been an assumption of mine that the house was around the corner or just out of view, not a serious hike up a hill, through a forest and down a meadow.

The first glimpse of the garden is of the Temple of Apollo, which is neatly positioned on the opposite side of the valley as you walk down from the house lawn and shrubbery. Inspired by the round temple of Baalbek in Syria, it was built in 1765 by architect Henry Flitcroft, who was contracted for most of the garden's structural works.

Many of the remaining structures throughout the garden have a distinctly Italian

CLOCKWISE FROM LEFT: a meandering gravel path around the great lake; a river was dammed to create the great lake at Stourhead; the Palladian bridge spanning the great lake is one of the more understated features of the property. Following pages: one of the 400-year-old oaks.

Lining the driveway up to the house are
400-year-old oaks, many of which are
hollow and now only exist because of their
cambium and a mountain of scar tissue.

LEFT TO RIGHT: in a garden close to the house, the lawn is ringed by a solid bank of hydrangeas surrounded by a mass of coniferous and deciduous trees; one wing of Stourhead, with minimal planting.

feel to them, inspired by Henry Hoare's European travels as a young man. At the bottom of the path and perched overlooking the great lake is the Temple of Flora, Hoare's first garden building, constructed over a natural spring and dedicated to the Umbrian river god Clitumnus.

An inscription above the door to the Temple of Flora reads 'Begone, you who are uninitiated! Begone!', a request from Henry that you only enter the garden in a happy mood. This sort of theatricality is rare in a garden and often forgotten in the modern landscape, more normally obsessed with being 'cool'. Artist Ian Hamilton Finlay's garden, Little Sparta (page 34), outside Edinburgh and started in 1966, is an exception.

The shore opposite the Temple of Flora is home to a hidden grotto. Often grotesquely over the top, grottoes are a feature I love, and the one at Stourhead continues the theme of Italian Renaissance mythological design. It is made from brick but lined with imported limestone and tufa. In the centre is a domed room in which lies a statue of a reclining nymph. At certain times of the day, beams of light pour into the room, lighting the creature. In a second room, a river god mounted on a rock points the way to Hoare's largest garden structure, the Pantheon.

Built in 1754, the Pantheon, one of the garden's most recognised features, holds the prime lakeside position. Visible from most parts of the garden and an excellent vantage point in itself, it held a very important position as an entertaining venue and destination. It was originally called the Temple of Hercules, after the large and quite confronting statue of the man-god that stands in the centre of the domed part of the building.

I, however, generally prefer subtlety over extravagance (in this case anyway) and consider one of the most beautiful yet understated features of the property to be the Palladian bridge. Well suited to the landscape, it provides the illusion that the lake is actually part of a river. It's not nearly as imposing as Brown's Palladian bridge at Prior Park, but requires subtlety so as not to detract from the garden's many other features. It's turf covered and rarely open to the public, but I've felt an overwhelming compulsion on my visits to run across from one side to the other for no reason at all.

Although it's full of extraordinary features, a garden, to me, still has to be about the use of plants. And, here, they certainly enhance the structures for which the garden is instantly recognisable.

I have seen some spectacular trees around the world but there are not many other gardens that can compare to the mature collection of Stourhead. There are tulip trees, handkerchief trees and ancient firs, but one of my favourites in the garden is actually a common old cypress, its sheer age contorting the tree into a 25-metre (81-foot) wide multi-trunked piece of Middle Earth ready to swallow you whole.

Many of the trees that appear in the garden today were not actually planted by Henry Hoare II, but are a legacy of his grand-nephew Sir Richard Colt Hoare. Richard was a scholar and historian and, after the unfortunate early death of his wife, he left for Europe for six years. What he brought back with him was a passion for exotic trees from around the world, which gave the garden texture and colour. He also started a collection of rhododendrons and gathered more than 600 cultivars and species

of pelargonium. The pelargoniums were a quaint idea, but his rhododendron collection ran wild and poses problems for the gardening staff to this day.

Richard left the property to his half-brother Sir Henry Hugh Hoare, the fourth baronet, who developed a passion for conifers and was responsible for creating the garden's collection of firs, spruce and exotic oddities. Some of his more outlandish plantings include the addition of western red cedar and giant sequoias, which are now the dominant tall trees in the garden.

It is the dream of any gardener to create a landscape that will be recognised and enjoyed through the ages. It is a sad fact, though, that often the person with the vision will not be the beneficiary of all the hard work. Gardens are never finished, further plantings need to be carried out and shaping is always required. In your own garden, you will always look at the faults instead of the big picture. I don't know if the garden at Stourhead would ever have made Henry II happy as he saw the result of his lifetime's work, but if he was the gardener I think he was, he would have most certainly enjoyed the constant challenge it presented.

Today, the garden at Stourhead requires two head gardeners, four full-time gardeners, the aid of two National Trust workers, an apprentice and the assistance of many volunteers. Its presentation and current aesthetic is attributed to their hard work and dedication. It is a very difficult job to maintain and create something as wonderful with so few but, with an understanding of how to develop a historic garden rather than to form one in isolation, the garden at Stourhead is an example of period garden style in action.

FOLLOWING PAGES, LEFT TO RIGHT: A river god in the grotto points the way to Hoare's largest garden structure, the Pantheon; built in 1754, the Pantheon, which holds the prime lakeside position, can be seen from most parts of the garden, and provides an excellent vantage point.

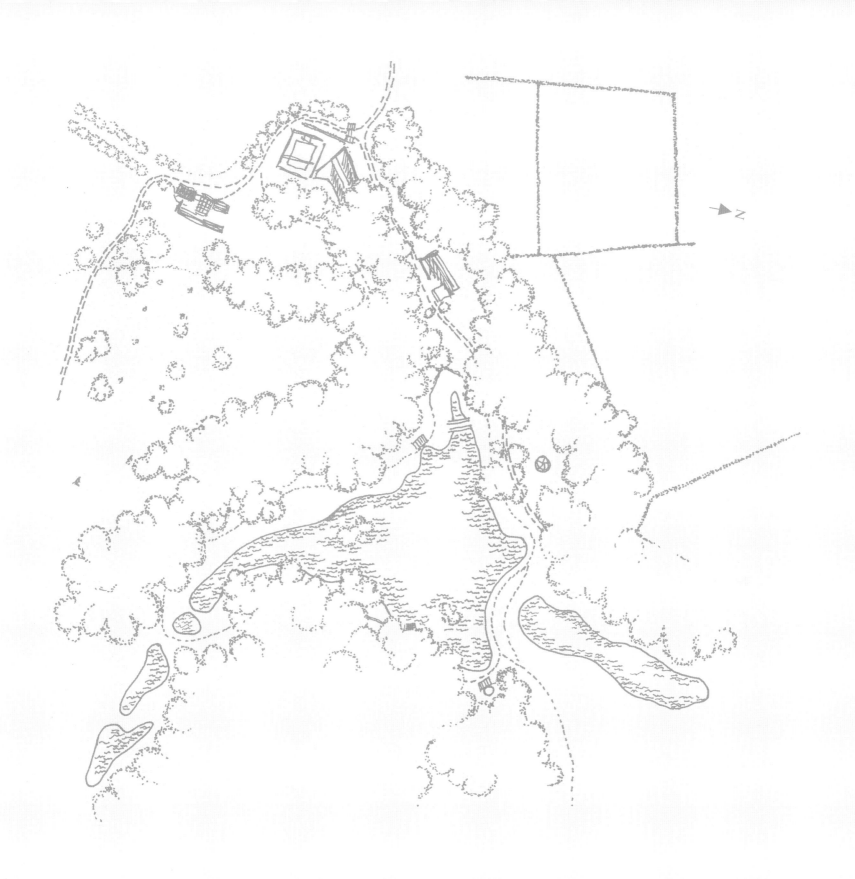

ARBORETUM

The basis of any Landscape garden is the arboretum, a most successful example of which is the grouping of trees at Stourhead. All the planting in the great garden is purposefully placed to direct the eye, to provide a backdrop or to be a feature in itself. By successfully trimming or training the trees, it's also possible to provide outlooks and controlled keyhole vistas. But the real design trait of the arboretum is the collection of species. In the past, the display of diverse specimens from around the world was an indication of one's own cultural depth and wealth, while in a modern garden the collection of varying species is important for the preservation of a broader genetic pool.

SCULPTURE

Far more difficult to install in the garden than most people realise, sculpture can either make or break a landscape. The fine carvings mounted on plinths on the front of Stourhead's Palladian entrance are beautifully detailed, providing a microscopic point of appreciation in what is generally viewed only as a greater expanse. Oddly, it is these details that will stay in visitors' minds, and although the garden may be one of the best in the world, if the sculpture had been bad, that would have had a hugely detrimental effect on the greater setting.

BENCH

While many of us would consider a garden bench as just a nice place to take a break – and there's nothing wrong with that – for others it can have quite a different purpose. One of my clients used his for business negotiations, the idea being to take the person he was trying to impress for a walk around the garden, talk generally as they were strolling along and then, as he was ready to close the deal, sit down on the bench, which had been strategically positioned in the most arresting spot. You need somewhere in the garden to get serious, whether it's a place to contemplate, do a business deal or woo a lover.

JACOBEAN (LANDSCAPE) GARDENS

FOLLIES

A garden should be fun. Some are even purpose-built as a haven for children to expand their minds and encourage creativity. The rest are built for big kids. As a designer, I receive a shopping list from my clients of all the things they want. Swimming pools, tennis courts, pavilions and pergolas are common requests, but for the adult spoilt child, a folly is the ultimate toy. No other garden in England has used follies as successfully as Stourhead. Henry Hoare's lakeside creations such as the Pantheon, shown here, are stunningly beautiful. His monolithic Alfred's Tower is pointlessly cool and the Temple of Apollo is, to say the least, a surprising punctuation in the landscape.

LAKES

A body of water serves multiple purposes. First, it keeps the garden watered. Beyond that, it provides a broad and open expanse – you can set things around it, but can't put anything actually on it, unless there happens to be an island in the middle. It's hard to know whether, centuries ago, people considered water views as the status symbols we do today, but as creating a lake is a major engineering feat, often requiring quite a serious dam, there's every chance they did. On a practical note, a lake regulates the temperature of the garden, having an ambient cooling effect, just as the harbour or ocean does. And with its reflective qualities, any nearby structure looks twice as impressive as it would do otherwise.

PALLADIO

The house at Stourhead is a wonderful Palladian mansion built in the 1720s. A design style inspired by the works of the sixteenth century architect Andrea Palladio, Palladianism became increasingly popular throughout the eighteenth century and right into the mid-nineteenth century. Many of the world's great structures are Palladian inspired: The White House in Washington, DC, and Edward Blore's renovation of the Buckingham Palace façade would probably be the best known. Throughout the garden at Stourhead, Henry Flitcroft built upon the Palladian influence of the main house with the Pantheon, the Temple of Flora and the Temple of Apollo.

Georgian (Picturesque) Gardens

In a Picturesque garden, low maintenance shrubberies become an integral part of the design, and the house becomes an important part of the landscape.

THE PICTURESQUE GARDEN is not a radical departure from its predecessor, the Landscape garden, but, rather, is a slightly more sensitive development of the philosophy. While Lancelot 'Capability' Brown went through a landscape, destroying what he didn't approve of, Humphry Repton (1752–1818), had a greater understanding of the possibilities of garden design. In Repton's world, not all gardens had to be fashionable – it wasn't either Renaissance or Landscape but, instead, a happy medium between the two, managing to add a few extra features as well.

For a start, the Picturesque garden typically looks far beyond its own walls to borrow whatever it can from the surrounding landscape. A nearby church steeple, for instance, can be framed to become part of the fabric of the garden. So, too, can a harbour view which, when seen through the branches of carefully placed trees, becomes far more interesting and appealing than one that's completely open and bald.

The house becomes part of the landscape in a Picturesque garden, with rooms opening to a terrace. Where Capability Brown would have cleared the beds and other structures from around the house, Repton was more likely to create areas of interest there. Brown would have picnics in the landscape, away from the house, while Repton, in a manner more relevant to today's way of life, would utilise the terraces near the house – you could say this was the start of the indoor/outdoor lifestyle.

The Picturesque garden is decorative – arboreta still exist, but are developed with a greater diversity of tree species. The meadow, such a part of English life, comes into its own in the Picturesque garden, and so too does the shrubbery, which has both a decorative and practical function, often acting as a screening device. People in those days were not quite as paranoid as we are today about privacy, but the shrubbery has always been used, to some extent, to block out one thing or another, and it's still an extremely effective way of doing so.

A shrubbery, made up of a collection of multi-stemmed, low-growing trees, makes absolutely perfect sense for many period gardens. Rhododendrons, which have very decorative flowers, are some of the most famous broad-scale shrubbery plants in the world, and despite being regarded by some as a weed, have remained an important landscape feature. Camellias are also extremely popular. In the great garden of Stourhead (page 58), cherry laurel has the dual function of acting as a supporting plant to hold together the hillside as well as being an understorey planting in the arboretum, adding a sense of scale to the trees.

Costwise, a shrubbery, although more expensive to establish than, say, a perennial garden, is much cheaper and easier in the long run, thanks to the minimal maintenance required and the exchange of plant materials possible. Although, in the past, a particular space may have been used for the planting of annuals, it is often not possible today, given high labour costs and a reduction in leisure time, to commit to such an endeavour, and that's where, again, the shrubbery can come in. Its maintenance will often require nothing more than small amounts of clipping, plus some regular feeding.

Another benefit of shrubberies is that you do have some measure of control. Where mature trees, in older gardens, often cast longer shadows than expected by the original gardener, shrubberies are a little more contained. Most are round in shape, with nondescript foliage, and rely upon flowers to provide a point of interest.

I have found that incorporating perennials into shrubberies is the best way to enhance fairly plain shrubs. In a shadier garden, supporting a stand of camellias with a perennial such as aspidistra or acanthus will provide the smaller foliage of the camellia with a contrasting material.

Shrubberies, first appearing in Picturesque gardens, have been used, more or less, ever since. As more exotic shrubs have made their way into our gardens, shrubberies have themselves become more interesting, not necessarily needing perennials for added colour and form. Mass planting is again an acceptable form of using shrubs in a period style garden. In his Spanish-inspired gardens, Russell Page, the renowned British landscape designer who trained as an artist before turning to the outdoors, relied upon more interesting specimens such as oleander, megaskepasma and hydrangeas in many of his designs. In the same way that arboreta now incorporate quite different trees from what would have been planted hundreds of years ago, so modern-day shrubberies can fit extremely comfortably into a period scheme.

A view from the vegetable garden towards the walled garden, one of many garden rooms at Haseley Court in the Cotswolds. The entry to the walled garden is flanked by a pair of pencil pines, and the wall is covered in cascading potato creeper.

The intimidating Georgian façade of Haseley Court calls for an equally dramatic terrace and forecourt, designed by Geoffrey Jellicoe. He installed a gravel drive and rectangular lawn, stone steps to the terrace and a yellow and blue border.

HASELEY COURT

Little Haseley, Oxfordshire

WHEN LOOKING FOR a new house, Nancy Lancaster was said to have visited more than 100 before settling on Haseley Court in 1954.

For £4000, Nancy had bought 32 hectares (80 acres) surrounding a Georgian-fronted house combined with a touch of Queen Anne, built upon the remnants of a mediaeval mansion. It sounds like the perfect house to me, but Haseley Court did have rather large shoes to fill. Nancy's previous residences included her childhood home, Mirador; Kelmarsh Hall, and the famous Ditchley Park – all coincidentally with landscapes designed by Nancy with the assistance of Norah Lindsay, Geoffrey Jellicoe and Russell Page.

Nancy Lancaster, described by renowned interior designer and gardener David Hicks as 'the most influential English gardener since Gertrude Jekyll', developed a wonderful garden around Haseley Court. In her later years, when she was unable to maintain the main house and a garden of such immense scale, she sold the property to live in a smaller house by the entry gate, and it was here that she created a spectacular garden inspired by her grander works. In the modest yard of the 'small house', she used clipped topiary surrounded by an amazing assortment of perennials and ornamental shrubs. The modern Haseley Court is a tribute to the work of Lancaster, developing as every garden should but maintaining the bones by which it was formed.

There are both macro and micro elements to the garden, an arrangement which provides the right blend of horticultural delights with the all-important 'wow' factor. The largest element, the formal drive and avenue, is a great example. Although the sheer expanse of the landscape provides a stunning view both to and from the house, it is still kept interesting on a smaller scale, with decorative hedging and accent planting at key locations.

I had the rare good fortune to be allowed to visit Haseley Court – which is not open to the public – with my friend Penny in a whirlwind tour of Cotswolds gardens. Prior to this, I had only ever had one visit to the English countryside. When I was 21, I went to the Royal Horticultural Society garden of Hyde Hall in Essex. It was a great garden, but at the time its biggest drawcard was that I could get there by train and a short walk, as I had little money and knew no one horticulturally minded in the UK.

Driving in the English countryside is an experience. Laneways suitable only for a single carriage are the access for all the great gardens, and Penny's confidence behind the wheel on such roads makes a visit to a garden even more enjoyable. It is, however, possible at any speed to miss the entry to Haseley Court. Drive by a simple gap in a hedge with a tunnelled drive of dense trees and shrubs and you've missed it. Whether or not this is an unfinished feature, I didn't ask, but not drawing attention to the

house from the street is at least a good way of maintaining some privacy and keeping unwanted guests away.

Haseley Court spans hundreds of years of architectural change. Some older Gothic walls of the mediaeval mansion have been pulled down, while others have remained. Gothic, Queen Anne and Georgian elements prevail, as the tastes of previous periods combine to form one spectacular structure. In a strange way, the simplicity of the Georgian architecture and details suit the older Gothic work, allowing the more detailed stonework to stand out against the blank straight walls of the more modern parts of the building.

Classically simple, clean and purposeful – in other words, completely Georgian – the grand entry to Haseley is all that a country manor should be. From this angle, the house is displaying its broadest, most intimidating stance, surveying all that is before it with a commanding stare. An eighteenth century planting of oaks outside the forecourt, flanking paddocks along the western vista, has recently been bolstered, reinforcing the dominance of the house over the surrounding countryside. Matching stone pillars topped with urns complete the setting, adding a formal punctuation point to the garden.

The equally dramatic yet simple western terrace and forecourt to Haseley were designed by Geoffrey Jellicoe. His design comprised a gravel drive that would encompass a rectangular lawn, generous stone steps to the terrace and a yellow and blue border planted for colour and scent, adjacent to the house.

The strong lines of the formal Georgian elements have been projected further into the garden, in the form of garden rooms and tree-lined vistas. The southern elevation of the house is a perfect example, where the symmetrical layout of the house is reinforced by strong yew hedges flanking east and west. The house and hedges combine to enclose a gravel terrace, which is not only a space for entertaining but also a viewing platform for a clever topiary design of symmetrically laid, clipped chess pieces. Made from yew hedging, in a sunken garden, they are arranged with the height of pieces scaling down towards the centre in a circular arrangement. This eccentric

the house and its setting in the landscape, and offers small vistas through to working fields. Vistas can be created from almost any structure, but scale is the important factor. The grand vista from Haseley Court is only possible because of the size of the structure. A smaller building could have a similar view but, in that case, it should start out more modestly in a framed fashion. An expanding vista can work much better in that situation.

In contrast to the formal yet, at times, eccentric layout surrounding the later architecture, the rambling nature of the older parts of the house have been matched with wild garden paths, meadows and perennial walks. The transition between the two occurs at gateways cut into yew hedging, essentially making garden rooms. On one side is rigid

perennial garden is a little more horticulturally biased, but still maintains a level of theatrics.

Repetitive buxus cubes are the dominating feature of the shaded perennial garden and mirror the theme of the box parlour, as too does taxus (yew), shaped like buttresses to support the mediaeval wall backdrop. Between the clipped evergreens, the beds incorporate shade-tolerant woodland perennials such as hostas and ranunculus. Significant changes to this part of the garden have taken place over recent times, simplifying it by reworking layouts and improving the colour schemes. The simplified garden now provides contrast to the shaded meadow on the opposite side of the path. Both the meadow and the shaded perennial garden have developed with the maturing of the surrounding trees, and it is obvious that this would have once been a very sunny space.

Adjacent to the garden is Lady Astor's canal, named as a tribute to Nancy's aunt, who often visited Haseley. Supposedly a former fishpond or moat, the canal is an excellent example of reusing existing features in a landscape and providing them with relevance. Old ruins, footings and pools can be used in a way that, more often than not, benefits the garden. Nancy realigned the canal with a significant beech at the far end and had a stone wall and tiered fountain constructed at the other. Today, the beech is no longer a feature, but a bench provides a focal point at the distant end of the pond.

The poplar grove behind the canal hides a small ruined temple. Nancy had originally planned a Gothic folly, in keeping with the nearby Gothic detailing of the house. As funding was a little short, she had it constructed from papier-mâché, but as it

From this angle, the house is displaying its broadest and most intimidating stance, surveying all before it with a commanding stare.

design, like the floral wheel in the stone garden, is one of the garden's signature features.

A topiary garden has supposedly existed at Haseley Court since the mid-1500s but, in its current guise, the garden dates back to 1850 and, in its current form, to 1900. The 100-year-old clipped garden's survival through times of war and abandonment is remarkable, to say the least. Part of that can be attributed to gardener Mr Shepherd, who had worked at the house when it was owned by a Colonel Muirhead. Shepherd would ride his bike from Great Haseley when the house was empty to maintain the topiary or, as he described it, 'clip [his] Kings and Queens'.

The current topiary design still has a sense of place that refers to the grandeur of

formality, on the other, natural randomness. I love the romantic nature of the more free-flowing, where one discovers rather than surveys. Finding what may lie at the end of a path or what surprise is around the next corner is very enjoyable.

The box parlour, predominantly a paved space of flint and mortared pebbles, is at the junction of Haseley Court's differing architecture, with doors and windows of both the Georgian and mediaeval components opening onto it. It's an entertaining garden of 'overfed' topiary pheasants, cloud shaped buxus and a wall of rambling purple and white wisteria that works perfectly with the architectural differences and continues the fun of the chess garden. The neighbouring shaded looked convincing, she told her horrified children she had had it carved from stone, dipping into their inheritance. (David Hicks, another great gardener, was also fond of theatrics, with one of his favourite tricks being the constant re-positioning of a plywood pyramid in paddocks around his house.)

During renovations or construction of pathways throughout Haseley Court, continuity of materials has been maintained. Grey/white pebble crush is used on the drive and large pedestrian areas, while the more intimate paths are treated with stone flagging and flint stone borders. Interestingly, although gravel, a cheaper substitute, becomes a solid mass when used on a large scale, for more detailed paths, the material needs to be of a larger format to achieve the same effect.

One particularly large part of the garden at Haseley is isolated from the architecture by hedges and tall walls. Although it is a space where it would be possible to become sidetracked, it still maintains a sense of place. Divided into four rooms and surrounded by hornbeam tunnels, the garden to the north of the house was originally a walled vegetable garden, or really a semi-walled garden, as the stone and brick walls only existed on the southern and western sides. Nancy originally asked Russell Page to redesign the space but found that his work was not to her liking, and instead decided that half the space would be ornamental and the other half agricultural. The final design saw the garden being divided again into quadrants. The south-western corner was retained as a highly ornamental vegetable garden, containing not only edible plants but also roses, peonies and iris. A fruit garden was established in the north-western corner. A white garden was built in the

TOP: the grand vista from the house is lined with oaks, most of which were planted in the eighteenth century, but with more added in recent years. Below: a potted brugmansia sits in the gravel courtyard. Following pages: the topiary chess pieces have existed at Haseley Court for a century.

CLOCKWISE, FROM TOP LEFT: the rear courtyard, showing the coach house that Nancy Lancaster moved into, and the magnificent horse chestnut; ornamental urn over an entry to the walled garden; a gate in Nancy Lancaster's last garden; the extension with knot garden in the courtyard.

north-east and the stone garden was constructed closer to the house in the south-east. Over time, these areas have largely been simplified, with lawns replacing beds, still resulting in huge planted, but more easily maintained, spaces. The stone garden and its feature bi-colour box wagon-wheel design and fish hook twirls have survived, and although not my favourite element, you have to admire the patience required to create and maintain it.

At the centre of the garden is an interesting timber pergola with a slated bell-shaped roof. I had seen the design in an American garden book – it turns out this actual pergola and garden have been the inspiration for designers all over the world.

The L-shaped hornbeam tunnels provide a clean simple backdrop to the four gardens. Inside the tunnels it's actually really dark and I could imagine a bit creepy for a small child. A grotto in the wall of the library provides a focal point for the east–west axis while a faded mirror at the end of the north–south axis creates a ghostly impression of your own reflection as you walk towards it.

Much of the beauty of the design lies in the way in which the tunnels act as corridors or extensions of the house, providing openings into carefully arranged rooms of colour and texture. It's similar to Nancy's work as an interior decorator. Many garden designers, including myself, have an affinity with interior design. The basic principles of design are exactly the same. Colour coordination, texture and scale apply to both disciplines and while interiors are not as dynamic as a garden, a well lived-in house isn't that far behind.

An often missed room flanking the northern side of the walled garden is the orchard. Merely cherry trees in a meadow, its simplicity and contrast to the dark tunnels are the key, making it a romantic and unexpectedly sunny space.

It was when I was in this part of the garden that I met the gardeners. A New Zealand couple who had been keen professional gardeners in the Land of the Long White Cloud, they had travelled to the UK for a change in pace, and are now living and working in one of the most spectacular gardens in the world. I'm a little jealous.

A recent addition has been a glasshouse and reconfiguration of the garden yard. Plant propagation and the development of collections are important for a large garden and it is only when you have the readiness of a dedicated space that a garden can be successful. Living in Sydney, I don't have the same need for a glasshouse and, as a visitor to the UK, I have learnt that it is best not to mention this. It can be demoralising for gardeners who have toiled to keep a specimen alive all winter to discover I have similar plants sprawled over my compost heap. The glasshouse at Haseley is a necessity and, while it is a modern construction, its siting within the period stone walls of the garden yard assimilates the structure into the landscape rather than showcasing it as a new installation.

Framed between the roomed gardens and the Queen Anne section of the house is a horse chestnut in a circular lawn surrounded by a gravel drive. The drive is the more informal access and the one preferred before inception of Jellicoe's forecourt design. The simplicity of the space has functional value but also enhances the aesthetics of the building, as the structure can be appreciated for what it is rather than being disguised behind layers of plant material.

In civic landscapes it has often been the practice of heritage architects to address the siting of historic buildings within modern landscapes by simplifying their surroundings, the idea being that the structure can stand alone and be appreciated without conflicting elements. I can understand this, but don't always feel it necessary. In some cases, isolating the structure from the landscape will make the building alienated in its surroundings, leaving the public unable to understand its purpose.

The old brew house, originally built in 1750, is located at the end of the gravel drive and court. Originally a two-part building, the brew house was added to by Nancy to create a third northern building, which matched the existing southern structure. She later added a tower to the central building to complete the design. The now symmetrical array of buildings was then converted to a laundry and orangery. Between the buildings, Nancy made a knot garden, featuring standard lonicera in the corners. Later, when Nancy moved to the coach house, she converted the orangery to a library. The collection of buildings has since been converted to a flat, which is rented to probably the luckiest tenants in the Cotswolds.

In Martin Wood's book on Nancy Lancaster, he writes about her asking her friend Billy Delano if he could define the word 'taste'. She wondered whether it was 'passing fashion only' or if it had 'a more definite quality'. Delano replied that taste was 'nothing more or less than a sense of appropriateness'. Nancy's beliefs were of the same persuasion and it is because of this that the garden is so successful. Period garden style isn't about imprinting your own tastes upon a landscape; rather, it's about working with the architecture of the day to create something special.

GRAVEL

Gravel is a handy product to use in the garden. It's inexpensive but manages to look a million dollars. But even more than looking brilliant, it also, for some reason, instantly sounds rich – maybe it's because many of the grand houses of the world have gravel driveways and paths. There's nothing quite like the sound of walking, or driving, on gravel. It's especially impressive when first raked – it looks good, too, that way – for when compacted, it loses its aristocratic crunch. So, one of the last tasks before guests arrive, of course, is to give the gravel a good raking.

GARDEN ROOMS

One of Nancy Lancaster's great strengths was her ability to create beautiful rooms, which she did very successfully in the house at Haseley Court. That skill spread to the garden which is, essentially, a series of rooms, each decorated differently and each with its own very distinctive and slightly quirky character. The grand forecourt (A), when you think about it, has walls and a floor, decorated with a rug in the middle (the lawn), with the gravel drive being the floorboards at the edge. The topiary garden (B) is incredibly busy – it's overdone and contains a ridiculous amount of furniture, but that's fine because, as contrast, there are beautifully simple rooms with 'walls' of hornbeam hedge.

SYMMETRY

The symmetrical nature of Georgian architecture can simply be transferred to the garden, and is an easy way out for anyone who's not expert in design. As in interior design, though, too much symmetry can be slightly stiff and formal, so it's important not to overdo it, and to be careful in the choice of materials and sense of scale. At its best, symmetry is entirely appropriate and extremely successful – working with asymmetry, opposing various elements against each other, and playing with scale, position and form does take more of a creative and artistic eye.

in detail
GEORGIAN (PICTURESQUE) GARDENS

FRAMING

In every great garden, there's at least one vista I'd have to call the 'money shot'. It often arises from something symmetrical – in this case, the pair of potted hostas halfway along the path, perfectly framed by stunning foliage forming a canopy across the view. There's a body of water there, too – now only a channel, but thought to be the original moat. And, as with all great views, there's a focal point at the end, which happens to be the simplest and cheapest garden bench possible, proving that each element doesn't have to be particularly remarkable in itself. The thoughtful and skilful way they're combined is far more important.

TOPIARY

There are not many garden features that amaze the masses as topiary does. Completely directed by fashion and a way of expressing the owner's personality, a topiary garden can be subject to reverence or ridicule. The topiary chess set at Haseley Court is one garden that has stood the test of time. One of the oldest garden features on the property, it holds pride of place beside the terrace of the drawing room. All the pieces have been shaped from *Buxus sempervirens* (English box) with the larger chess pieces surrounding the pawns.

MEADOW

Meadows are more common in Europe than in Australia – with the number of snakes in Australia, wandering through one could be dangerous. As a gardener, I look at a meadow and think, 'That looks fantastic, I don't have to mow it.' There's also something emotive there – it's the first sign of spring and instantly has an old-fashioned look. It's gardening at its most basic; grab some seeds, chuck them over your shoulder and see where they land. The results are often better than a rose garden or a clipped hedge, both of which take an enormous amount of work. You can't just plant anything, though – make sure colours don't clash, so go for the subtle or pastel.

VICTORIAN (GARDENESQUE) GARDENS

Coming from an age more associated with conservatism, the Victorian garden
has as its focus the exotic, unabashed and extreme.

During the Victorian era, the world suddenly became a much smaller place. Travel became easier and quicker and slightly less dangerous – and, as a result, people became fascinated by anywhere outside Europe; the more far-flung, the more appealing. That allure extended to gardens and so, in Europe, you may find a completely Indian garden or a garden made up only of African plants; as far as status symbols went, the collection of exotic plants was the equivalent of a batch of obscure stamps in the passport, a sign that you were well travelled and highly sophisticated. The broader your collection of plants, the further you'd ventured – your garden created a tangible sign of your lifestyle and place in society, a virtual record of your collecting trips. Extend that into the house, and if you could get hold of a stuffed lion or a bearskin rug for the living room, so much the better. After centuries of being limited by European plants, this was a time to break free and experiment.

That emphasis on the actual plants meant that in Gardenesque gardens the views became much shorter. There might be occasional keyhole views to the greater landscape, but even that wasn't completely necessary – the idea was to keep your head down and focus on the plants themselves.

It could have been because travel was still an adventure that the gardens of this period had a masculine sensibility to them. There was nothing delicate about the Gardenesque garden – it was bold; the colour schemes were vibrant, with orange, blue, burgundy, red, rust, yellow and brown being the predominant tones, with no pastels allowed; and the planting itself was in solid drifts.

A Victorian perennial garden is my favourite and, with its boldness of colour, form and plant selection, a basis for today's modern garden. Of course, it would be biased of me to say that the best Victorian gardens were in the colonies. The less severe seasonal weather and availability of exotic plant material ensured that gardens in the colonies became hosts to some of the greatest advances in horticulture. The garden at Bronte House in Sydney (page 104), with its rich colour scheme of burgundy, orange and purple, and backdrop of *Phormium tenax* and *Melianthus major* to support asymmetric groupings of salvias, crinums and ornamental grasses, is regarded by many as one of the best Victorian Gardenesque perennial gardens in the world, and a perfect example of how successful period garden style can be.

In the modern version of Gardenesque design, there's more of an emphasis on a structured approach, but it's still important to use a variety of strong colours; the word 'clash' doesn't come into it. You can think, as well, about an eclectic mix of plants that provide contrast in shape and texture – the silver-grey foliage of a *Dracaena draco*, for instance, providing a foil to the bright green of a cycad.

In Victorian times, you'd find meandering pathways; now, in the same type of garden, the path would curve on a radius rather than being so organic in its wanderings. The sorts of plants you might find include cannas, salvias, dahlias and lamiums, with maybe some lavenders, mints and sage as well. Perfume isn't necessarily a consideration but, if a plant does have a scent, it'll probably find its way to the entrance or near the front door. In superstitious Victorian times, quirky succulents were often placed near the house in an attempt to keep evil spirits away – whether they did any good, who knows, but they added another prized exotic touch to the surrounds. A Victorian perennial garden requires annual pruning and a major overhaul to have it ready for the next season – it does, on the whole, require a certain amount of looking after.

The main difference between a genuine Victorian garden and one re-created or developed today is that those exotic plants are no longer so strange to us – the plants that once so clearly indicated a life of adventure have now passed into common horticultural use and are easily available in nurseries virtually anywhere in the world. You have to work very hard nowadays to find the weird and unusual – I have managed it once, when I developed seeds from a worsleya, a plant native to remote Brazilian hillsides. As one of the seeds germinated and grew, I got a sense, for a while, of what it must have been like to be one of those Victorian gardeners, excited by every new specimen they came across. Now, most of us wouldn't have a clue where particular plants came from – they're so much part of our repertoire that we'd be surprised to know they started off in India or Indonesia or South Africa. While there's a lot to be said for having a wide range of plant material readily available, in doing so, we've lost something, and that's a shame.

One of a pair of very rare *Agave victoriae-reginae*, considered the collectors' agave, on the terrace at Rona in Sydney's Bellevue Hill.
For a Victorian gardener, collecting exotic plants from around the world was a sign of being sophisticated and well travelled.

RONA
Bellevue Hill, Sydney

PREVIOUS PAGES: the terrace at Rona. This page: the back of the house, with walls covered in Boston ivy and jasmine, faces towards Sydney Harbour. The perennial garden in the foreground features pink, blue and burgundy plants, a typically Gardenesque combination.

IT'S A RARE SITUATION in a city that anyone would attempt to enlarge a property in order to return it to its former glory. The sheer cost of land and the profits made on subdivision almost makes it a certainty that the great houses of the world are doomed to reside on smaller and smaller estates. When businessman and patron of the arts John Schaeffer bought Rona, he approached the purchase with more in mind than just a financial acquisition. He had the idea of restoring one of Sydney's great properties.

The approach to Rona is from a steep road in Bellevue Hill, a well-to-do Sydney suburb. The house is in the centre of the property, leaving only a stone wall, large gates and a small, medium-pitched roof visible from the street. Boston ivy, always kept clipped, shrouds everything, even the vertical bars on the fence and gate. First impressions are that this house is something special – unique and well looked after, yet with a measure of patina to hint at age and sophistication.

Rona was constructed in 1883 for the Australian industrialist Edward William Knox and his wife, Martha (Rutledge), and family. When he left school in 1864, Knox had joined his father's company, CSR (Colonial Sugar Refining), as a junior clerk, before rising through the ranks to general manager in 1880, steering the company to become one of the most profitable and broad-reaching businesses in the colonies. His beloved home, built at the end of the Victorian Gothic revival using sandstone quarried and milled on site, was more of a manor than a house. The Knox estate upon which Rona, with its high-pitched gables, was built was once 6.5 hectares (16 acres). Development over the years had sadly diminished the property to the point that,

when Mr Schaeffer bought it in 1989, the house and garden were only standing on 0.4 hectare (1 acre) of residential space.

The original property is chronicled in Helen Rutledge's book, *My Grandfather's House*. Looking at family photos, it's hard to believe that only 80 years ago, where there are now multimillion dollar houses, cattle grazed on meadows, driveways ran for more than 100 metres (325 feet) and most houses had woods, arboreta and expansive lawns.

Like many older houses, Rona has had a chequered past. Fire consumed it in 1905, causing severe damage throughout and entirely destroying the western wing. The central gable was removed in 1951 in an attempt to breathe new life into it, but left it only slightly smaller and with an open air courtyard in the centre. At one point, the house was subdivided into two, so two families could live in it, and later subdivided even further for use as a boarding house and classrooms for nearby Cranbrook School. Each change to the house

be suited to what he was aiming for at Rona. John was amazed at the diversity of plants, the period nature of Bronte and the colour we achieved from the garden. Although Bronte House is a mere cottage compared with Rona, the details on the timberwork, doors and windows were actually very similar to Rona's Gothic heritage.

Always guarded about the release of information, John's description of alterations was vastly understated. Since the purchase of the house, John had found himself with an opportunity to buy two surrounding properties. Both were once part of Rona and closer to the street, towards the southern side of the house, a section of the property that had become rather stuffy and cramped.

The first addition was the old stable, part of the original property entrance. Built at the same time as the main house, it had been sold and turned into a residence in 1959. The second was a derelict piece of land that had been excavated for a house but then

First impressions are that it is something special – well looked after, yet with a measure of patina to hint at age and sophistication.

did not enhance the architecture, and cheap renovations and minimal understanding of heritage saw Rona fall further into disrepair.

John Schaeffer bought Rona with the goal of reviving the house to its former glory. He fell in love with the architecture and position of the house, as well as its history. I met John at a function at Bronte House during my time working for Leo Schofield. John had recently finished some 'alterations', as he put it, to his garden and house and felt that what Leo and I had achieved at Bronte (page 104) would

left to its own devices. Combining all three blocks, John was able to construct a grass tennis court, surrounded by a thick screening of *Cupressus torulosa* and *Acmena smithii* (lilly pilly), and to create a link between the street, the stables and the main house at Rona by means of a new drive that passed through a forest of trees preserved from the days of Edward Knox.

The main drive into Rona is very special. It combines the heritage aesthetic with modern architecture while, at the same time,

preserving a strong horticultural presence. The significant tree plantings that form a cathedral-like canopy over the drive have a huge system of roots that fill every space in the garden. If the drive had been constructed over the tree roots, they might have suffered irreparable damage. Hence it was built from suspended concrete beams supported by a few piers, carefully placed so as not to disturb any significant roots. The end result is a drive that elegantly, in a very Gardenesque way, meanders through exotic trunks and buttress roots to open up in a leafy forecourt at the steps to the house.

Structural work on the property was a collaboration between heritage architect Clive Lucas and the garden design/construction duo Tony Ward and Inge Lee. Most new structural elements are a credit to Clive's work, including the Batcave-style garaging under the footings of Rona, which provides a modern solution without disturbing the heritage feel. Tony and Inge created privacy in the garden and much of its structure. Trees had been craned in to block prying eyes and to separate garden elements. Between the drive and tennis court, they installed several large Japanese maples, a Canadian maple, an ash and two conifers, one being a particular favourite of mine, the *Cupressus cashmeriana* or cashmere pine.

There was a slight issue with the garden, in that it lacked a sense of place. It wasn't something that could necessarily be requested if you didn't know what you were missing, but to me the garden at Rona required flair and horticultural adventurousness and specimens reminiscent of an age of eclectic exploration. The stunning trees of the entry garden, including *Agathis robusta* (Queensland kauri),

PREVIOUS PAGES: the driveway features an exotic mix, including cycads, silver maple and dracaena. This page: a bust of Diana in the conservatory, with Chinese star jasmine. Following pages, left to right: Diana, by Alexandre Falguière, on the lawn; hebes and hydrangea near the tennis court.

Araucaria heterophylla (Norfolk Island pine) and *Ficus virens*, definitely hint at what the garden was originally about.

A common mistake made by many in period garden design is that, although you may go out of your way to try and make a garden look 'old fashioned', you still need to pay attention to where you are. Rona has a very English countryside feel to it, yet we have a view of Sydney Harbour. That tells me this should remain a garden of multiple cultural influences, yet with a truly Australian feel.

My first work on the property revolved around the entry garden. Original photos showed that along the drive the Knox family grew weird and wonderful succulents like *Agave americana*. John also pointed this out and we developed a goal of purchasing and installing 'plants of interest'.

The prize planting was a mature *Dracaena draco* and a *Yucca elephantipes*. The two plants were found on a collecting trip to one of the mature tree sellers. The seven-tonne yucca was eight metres (26 feet) tall, with a buttressed trunk and multiple heads of foliage. The dracaena was only three metres (10 feet) tall, but had a classic umbrella shape with a four-metre (ten-foot) canopy. The yucca was craned in first and, along with a backdrop of palms and dark foliage, provided the perfect contrast for the dracaena. Placed on the tip of the forest garden, the dracaena caught all day sun, and was supported by clumps of cycads and a drift of silver plectranthus.

John's request for privacy in the garden provoked a number of vigorous discussions. Understandably, a private residential garden is a dream for many, but there are a number

of ordered stonework and organic rambling gardens. The feel is quite European but the plant choices of clipped hebes, hydrangea and elephant's ears put a Sydney spin on the display. Large *Camellia japonica* frame the entry to the house, and hints of fragrance are supplied by daphne and osmanthus.

The turning circle in the forecourt is not really a circle, but it's enough of one; the forecourt is made from white and grey stone chips, bordered by a small lawn, featuring two camphor laurels and a backdrop of lilly pilly. New steps and walls provide a formal border and stately entry. Large blocks of sandstone match the house perfectly, as do the sparrow-pecked and rock-faced detail.

John noted that the patina of the house needed to be replicated in the garden, and ordered the new elements to be scuffed up. To the horror of the landscapers and stonemasons, the walls and steps were whipped with a chain, and Boston ivy planted to further age the stone.

Rona's commanding position on the northern end of Bellevue Hill meant that it had one of the greatest views in Sydney. Standing in one spot on the northern terrace, it was possible to see 200 degrees, from the beachside suburb of Bondi, across all of Sydney Harbour and the entire city skyline. It is sad to say that such a view, which owners become precious about, has been the curse of many great gardens. Any designer who has ever worked on a waterfront or in a mountain position knows what I'm talking about. Something clicks and you want to be able to see the entire landscape from any position. This means that all planting is required to be no more than one metre (three feet) tall and the neighbours' trees had better watch out.

Understandably, a private residential garden is a dream for many, but there are a number of ways of screening without creating a wall.

Under the tall trees, the entry garden was very dark and contained a loose mix of ginger, clivia and camellias. I removed all the undergrowth and installed low retaining walls to gain much-needed planting soil above the tree roots. For planting, I laid all the material into drifts. Clivia was massed together, as were alpinia and hedychiums. New silver-leafed ctenanthe was installed for added colour, as too was the orange-flowering *Hedychium greenei*. I felt it was also important to remove any long vistas through this garden and, using Chinese fan palms, created a screen through the centre of the garden so that the displays could only be viewed when walking along the many paths.

of ways to obtain screening without creating a wall. One can plant a hedge or a row of something but, if the space allows it, layering is often a better option.

The short garden around the tennis court could only be screened with a hedge, which was made from *Cupressus torulosa* (I did dress it up slightly with clumps of angel's trumpet). In the forest garden, I removed the hedges to create a screen of clumping palms, specimen trees and large-leafed perennials. During the process, I was reminded regularly that we could still see the neighbouring blue roof, but in the end it was worth the effort.

In front of the house, my predecessors had done a good job of creating a stunning entry

The best views are framed and, fortunately, John knew and understood this. If you want to see what's behind the tree, you simply move. Framing the view to the east, John had planted an *Agathis robusta* several years before I began work on the garden. To the west, he kept the existing camphor laurels. This still left an expansive view through the centre of the property, in which we installed a mature New Caledonian pine. This form of araucaria is perfect in such a space; its habit is tall and pencil-like with an awkward lean that always points north in Sydney, a trait garden romantics refer to as the tree's longing to be sent home to New Caledonia.

The northern side of Rona receives all the sunlight. Perched right on the edge of a hill, the house has a sloping lawn that falls at 40 degrees to the bottom of the garden, giving the effect of the house almost being

stunted habit and white markings that look hand-painted, these two plants would be the ones to get hold of, and for a small fortune they were ours.

At the lower part of the lawn, I constructed a perennial garden in the likeness of the carriageway border at Bronte House. Burgundy flax forms the basis for the garden, while salvia and echium form the bulk of the fill. Rather than following an orange, blue and burgundy colour scheme, I moved further to a red, blue and burgundy scheme, drawing the red colour from the nearby rhododendrons.

It's only on rare occasions that you get the chance to work on properties supported by history, with owners willing to create something special, and something bigger than themselves. The work on Rona with John was such an occasion. John's passion towards art meant that there was always something

It's only on rare occasions you get the chance to work on properties supported by history, with owners willing to create something special.

on an altar. A mix of Boston ivy, jasmine and stephanotis covers the rear of the house. A port-wine magnolia adds a little asymmetric feel to the design, weighted away from the outdoor setting.

For many years, two Arts and Crafts stone pots at the rear of the house contained seasonal plantings put in by John's assistant, Pat. It wasn't that I wanted to do Pat out of a job, but following John's request for the weird and wonderful, I put out a call for unusual succulents for the urns. Happily, a man from Tasmania replied, saying he would be willing to part with his prized pair of *Agave victoriae-reginae*, the collectors' agave. Famed for its

interesting in the garden. Stone, marble and bronze statuary was placed throughout the property, working both as focal points and to give a sense of eclectic mystery. Even for a gardener who tries to make feature plants the focal point, it was difficult to compete and, therefore, in some places, the art and plants were required to complement one another.

I learnt a lot from working at Rona. I developed an interest in pre-Raphaelite art, for one thing, but mostly I learnt that a great garden can only come from teamwork between property owner and gardener, both focused upon a common goal. In this case, the goal was to create Sydney's best garden.

PREVIOUS PAGES: looking from the entry towards the tennis court, with hebe and camellia in the foreground and a stand of *Cupressus torulosa* in the background. This page: near the tennis court, a combined planting of clipped hebe, hydrangea, miscanthus and anemone.

BRONTE HOUSE
Bronte, Sydney

MOST GREAT GARDENS have developed over centuries. These gardens are dynamic landscapes that have evolved and been influenced by the different eras they have passed through. Fashions and tastes change and, because of this, many of these gardens have been twisted and reinvented, often losing their initial purpose and direction. Many colonial gardens are different, as the emphasis on preservation as they age is more common. Being an Australian, I have an obvious affiliation with colonial Georgian and Victorian gardens. My first job was at the Royal Botanic Gardens (RBG) Sydney and Government House, which are both predominantly Victorian. Located on Sydney Harbour, the RBG is the hub of Sydney horticulture. Originally the Governor's domain, its grounds have been a place for horticultural and agricultural endeavours for more than 180 years. Being surrounded by history and the aesthetic of such a grand landscape inspired me to learn and practise historic garden design, the backbone of my

Located in the oceanfront suburb of Bronte, it is a rare house for its time in that it was developed with the landscape in mind, in a location not established for agriculture or business but, rather, for relaxation and proximity to the sea. Most other homes of a similar ilk were constructed around the harbour and were attached to grand businesses. Their architecture was stuffy and, unlike that of Bronte House, didn't take advantage of the temperate Sydney climate.

Much of Lewis's work appeared on the high streets of Sydney. Rumour has it that he was stealing materials from colonial civic constructions to create Bronte House, and his return to England was somehow linked to this.

The architecture of Bronte House was revolutionary for its time. Small windows made way for large glass doors. Light was allowed to filter in, while extreme heat was kept at bay by large eaves and louvred shutters. The verandas were designed to be vast enough for outdoor entertaining and the house was positioned not only for a view of the Pacific but also to allow

Bronte House stood in the centre of a private oceanfront gully, which had its own beach and rock pool. A stream flowed from the escarpment above to provide fresh water for the house.

career. As luck would have it, my career as a garden designer and creator really started when I went straight from the RBG to work for Leo Schofield at Bronte House.

Bronte House was originally constructed by the colonial architect Mortimer Lewis and finished by lawyer Robert Lowe and his wife, Georgiana, as a retreat away from town. It is an example of Victorian Gothic architecture.

for cross ventilation. Once positioned on more than 17 hectares (42 acres), Bronte House stood in the centre of a private oceanfront gully, which had its own beach and rock pool. A stream flowed from the escarpment above to provide fresh water for the house. This abundance of water and its picturesque yet sheltered position made the location also perfectly suitable for a garden.

PREVIOUS PAGES: the carriageway and lawn outside the main entrance to Bronte House. This page: the carriageway border, a mix of European and subtropical plants, including crinum, melianthus, salvia and ginger.

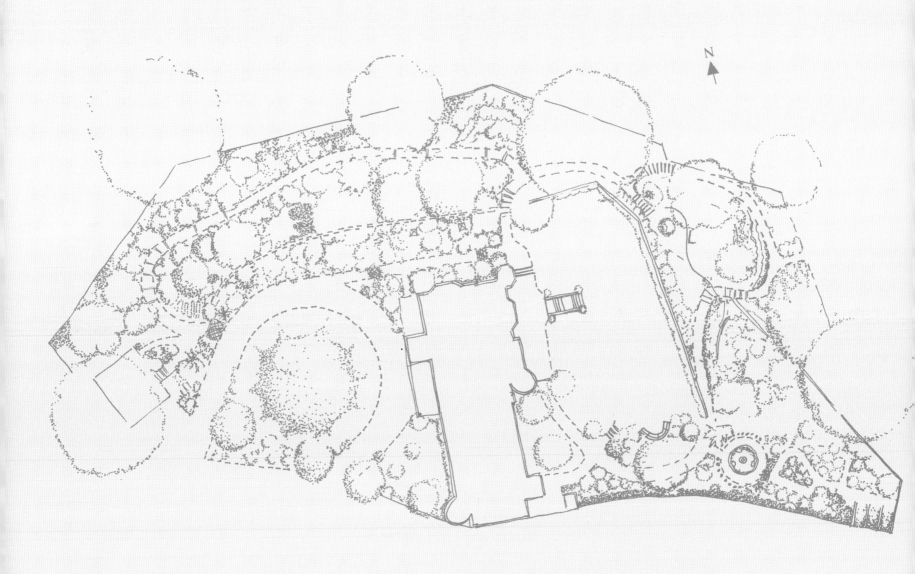

PREVIOUS PAGES: along the pea gravel pathway, the rose covered arbour is flanked by sentry plantings of hibiscus. The yellow and white perennial border contains a mix of plants, including canna, tobacco and giant strelitzia.

Georgiana Lowe was, without doubt, the driving force behind the garden, although there is no evidence to suggest that she made a garden proper as we would describe it. She did, however, establish picturesque walks, stands of trees, possibly a small orchard and a formalised drive, which at that time was the terminating point for Bronte Road. Sadly, the Lowes returned to England only five years after beginning their life at Bronte, and Georgiana's garden was not realised to its full potential. JB Hobbsworth purchased the property in 1865, and in 1895 sold most of the land as a rapidly growing Sydney was now knocking on the doors of its maritime landholdings. To develop the suburb, the road that once terminated at the doorstep of the house needed to continue further down to the beach. The once majestic property with its long tree-lined walks was reduced to a mere 0.7 hectares (1¾ acres).

Another side effect of chopping up the estate was that the house also received some harsh treatment. The sandstone cliff, from which the house is constructed, actually stood metres from its service entry. Rather than excavate into the hill to continue the road further down to the beach, a financially motivated decision was made to remove the south-eastern corner of the house. As some form of compensation, the stones of the destroyed elements of the house were recycled, creating a small second storey wing, with the end result forming a kind of terrace façade.

Subsequently, the landscape of Bronte House was chopped and changed, and it now bears no resemblance to the garden on the day it was conceived. Unlike other landscapes that have developed from humble beginnings, and been lost and then reinstated, the garden at

Bronte needed a new approach. It wasn't until 1994 that it received the careful attention that Georgiana had given it all those years ago. Leo Schofield, festival director and arts patron, had been an avid gardener for many years. His fondness for antiques and history had also been a prominent part of his life, and when the opportunity arose to purchase the lease for Bronte House, he jumped at the chance.

mystery and revealing absolutely nothing. The narrow pedestrian gate is unassuming, as is its location in the suburb. Many visitors and even locals of Bronte have wandered by oblivious to what is behind the fence. When working on the property, it is not uncommon to come across local kids taking turns standing on each others' shoulders to see what's going on in the 'Old Bronte House'.

The Victorian era was an exciting time: Queen Victoria's far-reaching grip on the globe meant that trade flourished between varying cultures and, importantly for gardeners, varying environments.

The planting scheme at Bronte has been about creating something flamboyant, while still maintaining the overall aesthetic of a traditional Victorian Gardenesque landscape. Luckily, a Victorian Gardenesque landscape in colonial Sydney had the hallmarks of something traditional with a twist of the exotic. Horticulturally, the Victorian era was an exciting time for the British colonies: Queen Victoria's far-reaching grip on the globe meant that trade flourished between varying cultures and, importantly for gardeners, varying environments. Hence, we find in a colonial Victorian garden tropical crinums from northern Australia side by side with gingers from Brazil and African tulip trees. The Victorians would have then combined these new-found exotics with common European perennials such as salvias, roses and buxus, the result being a period in gardening that is horticulturally and visually one of the most exciting in history.

The point at which you enter the garden at Bronte House has everything an entry to a garden should have, being somewhat of a

But this narrow entry masks a broad view that can only be described as a 'money shot'. Largely, the perennials in the carriageway border appear to be delicately positioned. Purple *Salvia mexicana* 'Limelight' and *Salvia* 'Black Knight' reside hand in hand with *Canna* 'Wyoming' and *Phormium tenax* (New Zealand flax). The flax is uniformly positioned and provides the garden with structure and contrast for lower plants.

Like most gardens, a Victorian garden is designed using formally laid-out structural planting. It's just that the type of planting used has an informal habit. In the carriageway border, *Phormium tenax* are planted at even intervals, providing a bold vertical accent from which more shrub-like plants can fall away. Flanking most of the flax are *Salvia mexicana* 'Limelight' and ornamental grasses, including *Miscanthus sinensis* and *Pennisetum alopecuroides*, along with smaller perennials and bulbs, including crocosmia, agapanthus and cheiranthus.

Although the garden at the front carriageway border displays a free-flowing form and habit, a strict colour scheme of orange, blue and burgundy has been maintained. All plants displaying yellow and white were left out of the carriageway perennial borders and planted on the sunnier, northern side of the house. It seems the lighter coloured flowering plants perform better in sunnier locations.

Intelligent design has meant that this side of the house has very few windows. Only the dining room has a bay window, but even then it is fitted with a louvred shutter. The shade cast by a large leaved senecio dapples the light into the room, while *Hedychium coronarium* (white ginger lily) is positioned to provide fragrance and naturally cooling greenery for the room. The combination of the architecture of the house and the garden design leaves the room cool even on the hottest summer days.

With no other doors or windows to consider, the abundant space has been filled with *Strelitzia nicolai* (giant bird of paradise), yellow brugmansia, *Salvia azurea* and *Hymenocallis caribaea* (white spider lily).

A feature of the drawing room wall is the *Thunbergia mysorensis*. A plant known more commonly in tropical gardens, this thunbergia flowers all year round and growth doesn't slow down during winter, thanks to the heat from the north facing wall along with that radiating out from the drawing room fireplace.

Georgiana Lowe's contribution to the garden provided the bones for what has been achieved today. Unfortunately, many of the more finite details of the garden have been lost. My predecessor at Bronte House, Brendan Lewis, who had, thankfully for me, done much of the hard work clearing and felling, stumbled across what he had thought of as a pile of waste stones and beach material. On closer inspection, it was found to be placed in an ordered arrangement, consistent with a rockery. After consulting the house records, letters were found from Georgiana stating that she had been collecting interesting material from the seashore and surrounding bush in order to establish a rockery garden.

When working on a heritage garden, such a find can be exciting or painful but, in this case, the rockery became the centrepiece for a significant succulent garden. Succulents themselves have long been on the receiving end of love-hate relationships with gardeners and the public. Perennial victims of fashion extremes, succulents have become popular again as 'designer plants', as modern landscape designers have finally noted that some which may seem gaudy have merit as architectural features. The Victorians saw succulents and cacti as amazing botanical finds and, in many situations, they became the prize of great estates. One particular agave with a perfect rosette of short green leaves bordered by fine chalky white lines even took on the name of the then ruling monarch to become *Agave victoriae-reginae*, the only other plant to do so being a giant aquatic lily, *Victoria amazonica*.

Inspired by the succulent collection at Bronte, I wanted to learn more and, while on a trip to Europe, made a detour to the Jardin Exotique in Monaco. The steep hillside garden, with its valleys filled with barrel cactus and trailing pigface, further inspired me to tackle a redevelopment of the Bronte succulent garden. Although it doesn't have a view of Garibaldi's castle, Bronte can be considered a microcosm of the great Monaco garden in its topography. One of the main keys to success with Jardin Exotique's displays was the positioning of the large feature succulents relative to the contrasting nature of the lower ground cover

LEFT TO RIGHT: the Jardin Exotique-inspired succulent garden features agave, frucrea and *Butia capitata*; a French pottery basket contains a collection of echeveria and sempervivum (houseleek). Following pages: a sea of aspidistra and Moreton Bay fig at the eastern end of the lovers' walk.

The eastern terrace, with clipped oleander to the left of the house. In the foreground, orange cosmos borders the bamboo fence. The lawn is Queensland blue couch, a very fine, high maintenance type of grass with a blueish tinge.

material. Giant blue *Agave americana* requires green or even red kalanchoe as a contrast colour, while large clumps of euphorbias are better displayed when surrounded with masses of chalksticks, *Senecio serpens*. Elevating the larger succulents closer to eye level also proves to be a successful endeavour, allowing the finer details of the plant to be noted. The whole display is an eclectic masterpiece worthy of any Victorian garden.

In the perennial gardens around the house, succulents such as the huge *Furcraea selloa* have been planted and interwoven with unrelated perennials to create an exotic twist. The thematic colour-coded design used in the perennial gardens has also been followed in the succulent plantings. By using species found in the agave genus, it is possible to find a variation to suit any colour scheme. *Agave stricta* sits perfectly in the yellow and white border, surrounded by day lilies and yellow flowering *Strelitzia reginae* 'Mandela's Gold', while the smaller orange-flowered echieveria are suitable for use around the carriageway border, contrasting with the lower sprawling ground covers.

Like succulents, orchids can also be adapted to massed collections rather than being just used as accent plantings. Adjacent to the succulent garden, an orchid collection takes pride of place. It's a perfect situation, really, with the ground too rocky and planting space too limited for plants with more common root growth. Many orchids have succulent qualities; some are even regarded as lithophytes, and that's perfect for this location. Horticulturally, we should work with plants that grow in the natural conditions we are given rather than waste time and money on changing our environment. The locally found

Dendrobium speciosum forms the centrepiece, with crucifix orchids and fragrant zygopetalum adding small accent features to the remaining crevices and stonework.

When the garden was reduced in size, a lovers' walk was lost to the outside world. The lower gardens at Bronte House include a new version of it, a dedicated subtropical walk. The protective cover has made the garden a haven for shade-loving species and there are many subtropical plants with large leaves suitable for such a job. One of the best is the clivia, which forms the basis of the lovers' walk, with specimens and clumps of assorted species planted into the drift.

Cyathea cooperi tree ferns through the back of the clivia bank, and stands of *Phoenix roebelenii* (dwarf date palms) through the front of each bed. This additional layer adds an extra dynamic, turning a hillside into a more Gardenesque aesthetic of exotic specimen plants and free-moving drifts. The trees in this area also provide that traditional Gardenesque feel and include *Phoenix canariensis*, *Araucaria heterophylla* and *Araucaria columnaris*.

Araucaria heterophylla, the Norfolk Island pine, is a common Sydney plant. *Araucaria columnaris*, the New Caledonian pine, is less common and far more spectacular, with the 30-metre-high (97-feet-high) tree leaning

Where possible, in Gardenesque, plantings should be exotic with the underlying idea of experimentation. But, overall, the garden needs to have a romantic undertow, with a sense of adventure.

Much of the work in the lovers' walk was carried out by Brendan Lewis. A tropical plant enthusiast, Brendan, under the guidance of Leo Schofield, planted a drift of *Alpinia zerumbet* (shell ginger) as a screen along the northern fence line to form a large screen, in front of which he planted the first of the garden's many clivia. One may even refer to it as the clivia garden as there are estimated to be more than 100,000 plants in this section alone. To add interest, large drifts of ctenanthe and *Hedychium greenei* provide contrast to the solid green of the clivia.

As a design, the drift of low perennials is impressive but it did initially lack structure. The advice that came from the great Victorian gardener Michael McCoy was that the garden would benefit from evenly spaced clumps of

northwards by 10 metres (32 feet). The tree itself is in keeping with the romantic nature of the garden, and sums up what Victorian Gardenesque is about. The garden is bold, with plantings using distinct colour and form. Where possible, in Gardenesque, plantings should be exotic with the underlying idea of experimentation. But, overall, the garden needs to have a romantic undertow; it need not have an expansive view but should be more of an adventure, to explore and discover gradually.

As part of the council requirements of tenanting Bronte House, residents are requested to open the garden six days a year. These open days, although a lot of hard work, are a rewarding part of working in such a landscape, allowing one of Australia's greatest perennial gardens to be enjoyed by all.

STEPS

The giant-sized steps into the subtropical lovers' walk from the upper part of the garden are remnants of an extension that was added to Bronte House. A spare room was formed by blocking in the conservatory veranda on the north-west corner of the house. This addition was removed during restoration work and the materials were then kept on site, and later reused by Leo Schofield as quirky steps to the garden beyond. Recycling existing building materials helps create uniformity between the house and garden.

SUCCULENTS

At a time when the world was opening up and the unusual was being celebrated, succulents became the ultimate exotic of the Victorian era. The most famed is even named *Agave victoriae-reginae* (above at Rona). The succulent garden at Bronte House is created on the property's free-draining rocky edge and contains a large array of feature agaves, aloes and frucreas surrounded by drifts of trailing succulents. Succulents have gone in and out of fashion over the years, but for those who appreciate their hardiness and strangeness, they'll always have a place in the garden.

CANNA 'WYOMING'

While in some senses, the Victorian era was considered conservative, that wasn't the case outdoors, where bold colour was crucial for the preferred, masculine garden aesthetic. To re-create that theme, use colours such as burgundy, purple and orange. This *Canna* 'Wyoming', with its burgundy brown leaves and orange flowers, forms a vital part of the carriageway perennial border at Bronte House. Associated in the garden with *Salvia mexicana* 'Limelight' and *Melianthus major*, the canna is not only a feature but also provides contrast by which other plants can exist and flourish.

VICTORIAN (GARDENESQUE) GARDENS

WEEDS

Many so-called weed species were prevalent in Victorian gardens, partly because they look good, but also because they are fast and easy to grow. Weeds, like beauty, are in the eye of the beholder. Lantana is a plant that used to be quite common in the garden but is now frowned upon, as too are species from the ricinus genus. Here in the perennial garden at the end of the eastern terrace at Bronte House, the strong burgundy tones of *Ricinus communis* 'Rubra' provide an injection of rich colour, and contrast with the pastel blues and mauve of the echium and lantana. The ricinus is let go to seed and cut down every year.

ECLECTIC

Rather like collecting stamps or coins, finding a species of plant and building a collection was a very Victorian pastime. Orchids and crinums were favourites and, far less exotic from today's point of view, so too were pelargoniums and geraniums. The conservatory at Bronte House has been developed from a collection of begonias. Mainly made up of cane begonias and *Begonia rex*, the collection is useful both as outdoor and indoor decoration. All the pots have been selected to make sure they fit into jardinières inside the house.

BAMBOO FENCING

Garden craft is a highly skilled and useful tool in any garden. The fence that surrounds the eastern terrace at Bronte House is created from the 150-year-old *Bambusa balcooa*, an edible type of bamboo reputed to have been imported into Australia from Cape Town with the First Fleet. The smaller stems were sawn to form straps and the larger stems split to create the capping pieces, which were then held to the top via rope and straps. The straps, acting like structural bracing, were screwed to hardwood supporting posts. The result is both rustic and nostalgic and perfectly in keeping with the style of house and garden.

Edwardian
(Arts and Crafts) Gardens

Edwardian gardens, with their perennial borders and pastel tones, are notably prettier and more feminine than their earlier counterparts.

THERE'S A TENDENCY to think of Victorian times as being conservative, but in many ways that's not the case, and certainly not when it comes to gardens. At a time when overseas travel started to become more possible, exotic species were grown and displayed as status symbols, and gardens became a living record or map of their owners' foreign adventures. Rather, it was the years directly following the Victorian age – the Edwardian period – that I've always considered a throwback. Until then, gardens were evolving, with ideas from previous eras adopted and improved upon. Whether it was the accelerating pace of change in the industrial world that put a halt to the development of the garden is hard to say, but the Edwardian period saw a reversion to tradition. At a point in which industry was moving into the countryside, and the handcrafted was making way for the machine made, there was a yearning for an idealised version of an earlier time. The Arts and Crafts movement grew out of that and invaded every part of domestic life, from the design of books to wallpaper to houses – all had a handcrafted look to them and a design to match.

That philosophy spilt over into the garden and the results, while being romantic in some ways, were also quite impractical. One reason I don't like genuine Edwardian gardens is that they were overdone – if there was any way to make an area more complex, it would be done. That could mean adding a birdbath, fountain, sundial, some garden gnomes or even a couple of stone figurines of Ratty and Mole from *Wind in the Willows*. When I was doing the Ingleneuk garden in Sydney, we kept digging up carved frogs – the worst type of Edwardian garden is quite kitsch, and too jam-packed to be able to use comfortably. If you're planning an Edwardian style garden now, there are authentic elements you can use, in terms of plantings and of decorative paraphernalia, but the best advice would be to show restraint – this is a case of less being more.

For the first time, the ornamental garden was not just the domain of the ultra-wealthy – with increased leisure time, even the working class had time for their plots. And seeds were easier to get hold of; gardens no longer mapped out the owners' travels but, rather, illustrated their taste or lack of it. While gardening itself might be a leisure pursuit of the working class, the well-to-do wanted more than that, building croquet lawns and tennis courts to further enhance their lives. Spending time outside in the garden was expected, and thus created a boom in the outdoor furniture market. Around the Mediterranean, you can find quite a lot of concrete furniture cast in the shape of timber logs – an interesting mix of industrialisation with a natural leaning; elsewhere the rustic 'twig and stick' furniture, looking as if it could have been put together in someone's shed, was found in many back gardens.

Edwardian gardens were prettier and more feminine than their forerunners, containing many more flowers which, given this was the age of the doily, tended towards the delicate and lacy. Typical perennial borders would be made up of plants like hellebores, hostas and aquilegias, and then you'd find hydrangeas, gardenias, rhododendrons and camellias, all in pastel tones, as well as spring-flowering bulbs. They'd usually be planted together in a riotous mix – the idea of drifts of one sort of plant wouldn't fit into the scheme.

Symmetry plays only a minor role in this type of garden – there might be one tree on either side of the house or a pair of trees framing the entrance drive. The planting of an avenue of trees was very popular, too – the types of trees you might use now include the prettier ones like oaks, elms, horse chestnut or any of the other European varieties.

Paving, like a lot of the other features of an Edwardian garden, has a handmade look to it – crazy paving and random flagging were very popular, with rough edges to the sandstone, slate or limestone rather than a sharp-edged sawn finish. Perennials would spill out of cracks and crevices in the paving – spontaneity and chance were so much part of the way of thinking. Another possibility for pathways is gravel, another very popular but quite understated choice.

Walled gardens were a common feature of Edwardian gardens and, while they can be very appealing, they more often than not fail to take the surrounding countryside much into account. There could be the most spectacular view beyond the walls, but you wouldn't know it. That's typical for gardens of the time – there was a tendency to become immersed in what was right there in front of you rather than having a view of the larger landscape. Again, that was probably tied up with the inward-looking nostalgic mood of the time.

Wildlife among the perennial borders at Hodges Barn, a Gloucestershire garden with a definite Arts and Crafts feel that is made up of a series of appealing garden rooms and built around an unusual fifteenth century house.

PREVIOUS PAGES: a view of one of the towered dovecotes at Hodges Barn. Entry walls were built by Italian prisoners of war. This page, clockwise from left: the perennial border has an Arts and Crafts feel; entry from the formal garden to the greater landscape; a resting spot.

IN CREATING A period style garden, it is always good to research the architecture at the centre of the landscape, for this is where you will find your inspiration. Some buildings are easy to pigeonhole into a particular period; for example, pointed arches and multi-paned windows would tell me that it is a Gothic-inspired building, while a house in the suburbs with no eaves, plain rendered walls and poor building quality is a modern McMansion. On other buildings, you may need to research stone design, brick type and bonding, or a host of other architectural details. Some buildings, however, are very difficult to categorise.

Crafts overtones now reflected in the garden – has had a new life as a family home.

A quirky house needs a clever and original eye to create a successful garden. And an interesting structure needs a garden that isn't dominated by that structure but, rather, works with it to be mutually beneficial. The garden at Hodges Barn is a tribute to great design and perseverance.

When I visited Hodges Barn, I was amazed at the way the garden rambled from one area to another in an ordered yet very relaxed manner. A photo of the house had once graced the front cover of the English

of the house. The tradesmen's entry to the house is via a path through the ground cover.

Amanda Hornby is a passionate horticulturalist. She has a brilliant eye for colour and arrangement, and can see the value in trying something different. We set off from the forecourt and into a shrubbery border supported by background plantings of horse chestnut and copper beech. The purple tone of the beech is quite prevalent in the garden, with strong splashes of burgundy from berberis. The garden in its entirety is surrounded by a yew hedge and continues the garden room theme, a feature for which the whole of Hodges Barn is noted.

Garden rooms are a very good design element. They allow the designer to experiment with different themes, such as colour arrangements, plant types or even microclimates. I like the garden room idea at Hodges Barn because the building was once an agricultural structure, and the garden rooms continue the lines of the building in much the same way as the yards of an old barn. The design also plays on certain noted features of the house. The formal entry side of Hodges Barn runs an axis into the garden, flanked by a symmetrical design of Scottish yew clipped into columns, terminating at a garden bench.

This garden room is open and relies upon the dramatic simplicity of the yew columns and a beautifully detailed tapestry hedge. Such a hedge is only for the horticulturally astute as it involves growing plants of often differing growth rates and aesthetics as one single organism. This one is a combination of yew, thuja, beech and holly, and is designed to be a point of interest in both winter and summer.

A great garden is more than something to look at. A great garden should provide the

I was amazed at the way the garden at Hodges Barn rambled from one area to another in an ordered yet relaxed manner.

Thumbing through David Hicks' book *Cotswold Gardens*, I came across Hodges Barn, an unusual fifteenth century house with a stunning garden. The house was a rough rectangular shape, symmetrical, with three windows top and bottom on both sides, and a door in the centre. The walls were constructed from random limestone rubble mortared together like brickwork, while detailed carved stone sills surrounded the windows and doors. The roof was, however, a little different.

On both the front and rear of the building, a square domed tower is the main feature, each looking a bit like a silo. David Hicks referred to the building as once being a columbarium or dovecote, the two towers apparently holding pigeons bred for the table of the nearby manor. The owner, Amanda Hornby, confirmed this and with the nearby manor now gone, the barn – the interior of which has definite Arts and

Open Garden catalogue and, although the house is no longer ever open to the public, it is almost constantly ready for such an occasion. The level of detail was astonishing, and the arrangements which the talented gardener-owner, Amanda Hornby, had developed were refreshing and bold.

The drive leading towards Hodges Barn is quite romantic, dipping and turning with the contours of the land, approaching the house side-on like a building perched on the side of a street. The drive, although continuing through to garages, officially stops at the house, with the entry into a garden room. Feeling more like a garden than a driveway forecourt, this part of the house is the first opportunity to get a really good look at the unusual rotund dovecote towers. On the ground, though, the garden aspect is emphasised by a drift of geraniums and heuchera, extending off from both corners

LEFT TO RIGHT: each walled garden at Hodges Barn is influenced by the immediate contours of the garden and its relationship to the house but, with breaks in walls, also relates to the surrounding countryside; willow on the banks of an informal pond in the water garden.

visitor with a sense of euphoria as they pass from one area to the next. Hodges Barn is a visually exciting garden, and one of the few landscapes I have ever been in which inspires those feelings. It is also a garden that, thanks to its garden room design, builds anticipation. Not being able to see into the next space, but having the knowledge that the thematic design of each room changes, is an exciting prospect.

One of the beauties of a walled garden is that how or what you let the guest see is up to you. A cleverly designed garden creates voids directing the attention away from spaces that seem undesirable or utilitarian. At Hodges Barn, a tour around the garden rooms may quite naturally focus upon the spectacular planted areas, and a visitor may be excused if they don't happen to come across the swimming pool, tennis court or kitchen garden with potager.

The working parts of the garden and the more modern entertaining areas are well hidden, as well as being beautifully presented in their own garden rooms. Heading from the open tapestry hedge, it is possible to enter the growing yards and glasshouse and then the vegetable garden. Far from being purely a place for propagation, the garden contains many decorative features as well as the required assets for subsistence farming. I particularly like the use of the woven willow fences and the patterning created on the pea stands. I actually tried to create similar ones in Sydney at Bronte House and failed miserably.

This garden surrounds a tennis court, which is a problem in most gardens. Tennis courts are large blank ugly spaces, but here a tennis court fence is just another wall waiting for a feature and, in this case, has been used as a frame for growing espaliered fruiting trees.

Vegetable gardens are very hard work. Although they may seem a great idea, they don't often receive the treatment they need. When Amanda saw she no longer required as much vegetable garden space as she used to, she decided the design wouldn't alter but the plant type would. Half the garden is now made up of the familiar rows of a working garden, while the other half is a meadow.

The tennis court at Hodges Barn abuts onto a pavilion, which doubles as a swimming pool house for a very private garden room. Almost missed on the tour, the pool is a perfectly proportioned, rectangular body of water. Surrounded by stone walls and an orchard in a light meadow, the pool works not only as a recreation space but also as an area for relaxation. Pot plants take the stark edge off the paving, and the proximity of the garden prevents the pool from being a single-use white elephant in the garden.

My favourite garden room is, however, the water garden, created around an informal pond. The pond contains fringe plantings of iris and *Hosta sieboldiana* var. *elegans*. A willow hangs into the water and spot tree plantings provide a wooded yet open feel. The natural contours of the land have been kept in this part of the garden, which is an interesting change from the structured smaller rooms in the other parts of the landscape. One feature I like is the way the garden relates to the house. Unlike the area at the front of the house, where the garden is aligned with the axis of the dovecotes, this garden is relaxed and, in many ways, echoes the relaxed nature of the house. The multiple roof lines and chimneys are perfectly suited to the landscape.

Stone walls, many of which were constructed out of paddock stone by Italian prisoners of war, form much of the backdrop to this garden. Roses such as 'Iceberg', 'Kiftsgate' and 'Bobbie James' now cover the walls, a legacy of Amanda's husband, Charlie.

The more natural setting of the water garden is supported by the adjacent wood, containing both mature and newly planted trees, and created by the Hornbys just outside the garden proper. Entry is via a lovely timber gate in the stone walling. Although it's quite charming, Amanda's preference would be for no gate at all, and to have a seamless flow into the woods. This gate, however, has a dual purpose as the first line of defence against badgers and burrowing animals.

After working in the country, I know what it means to keep pests like rabbits out of the garden. However, being an Australian, I've never had to deal with a badger problem. I can be sympathetic, though, as I have, in the past, lost a whole garden to a wombat, and hundreds of trees to kangaroos. If only it was as simple as closing the gate to keep them out!

For those who love symmetry, the formal garden on the southern side of the house is a favourite feature. Perfectly framed from one of the dovecotes, the garden is a vibrant mass of colour, with red and pink roses, salvia, euphorbia and geranium. A terrace by the house adds further interest with its detailed stonework around the garden door. The surrounding walls have been aligned with the main axis of the house as, too, has a grouping of trees at the end of the garden before the view disappears into the countryside.

How a garden relates to the greater landscape is important. Most good design blends seamlessly from garden to landscape, often using what is referred to as a 'borrowed view'. Typically, a walled garden could be

CLOCKWISE FROM LEFT: gateway into the woods acts as the first line of defence against badgers and burrowing animals; drive follows the contours of the land; Scottish yew clipped into columns forms an avenue leading towards the front door.

A great garden provides the
visitor with a sense of euphoria.

excused for not relating to its surrounds, as by definition it cuts itself off from outside influences. Here, however, we have the best of both worlds – each room is thematically planned to have a certain feel, influenced by the immediate contours of the garden and its relationship to the house. By using breaks in surrounding walls and lower fence heights, each perimeter garden also relates to the countryside. The central axis of the formal garden borrows the adjacent paddocks as an infinite backdrop, while the pond garden uses a cleverly laid-out arboretum to blend into neighbouring trees.

I like every part of the garden at Hodges Barn – the horticultural nature of the design, the changing garden rooms and thematic styles. It's just a wonderful garden to be in.

I like every part of the garden at Hodges Barn – the horticultural nature of the design, the changing garden rooms and thematic styles.

It had rained the night before Amanda Hornby took me through, so any problems in the garden relating to that were excusable. In true gardener's form, though, she apologised for the state of the garden and weather before I had even had a chance to look around.

The garden was immaculate, of course, but it made me realise that the trait of a great gardener is to not see their creation as it should be viewed. A great gardener is happy to be making a landscape, and is almost never completely content with their work.

PREVIOUS PAGES: ordered chaos in a perennial garden demonstrates the owner's mastery of colour and arrangement. This page, top: a framed view of one of the former dovecotes. Below: a seat tucked into the clipped buxus hedging.

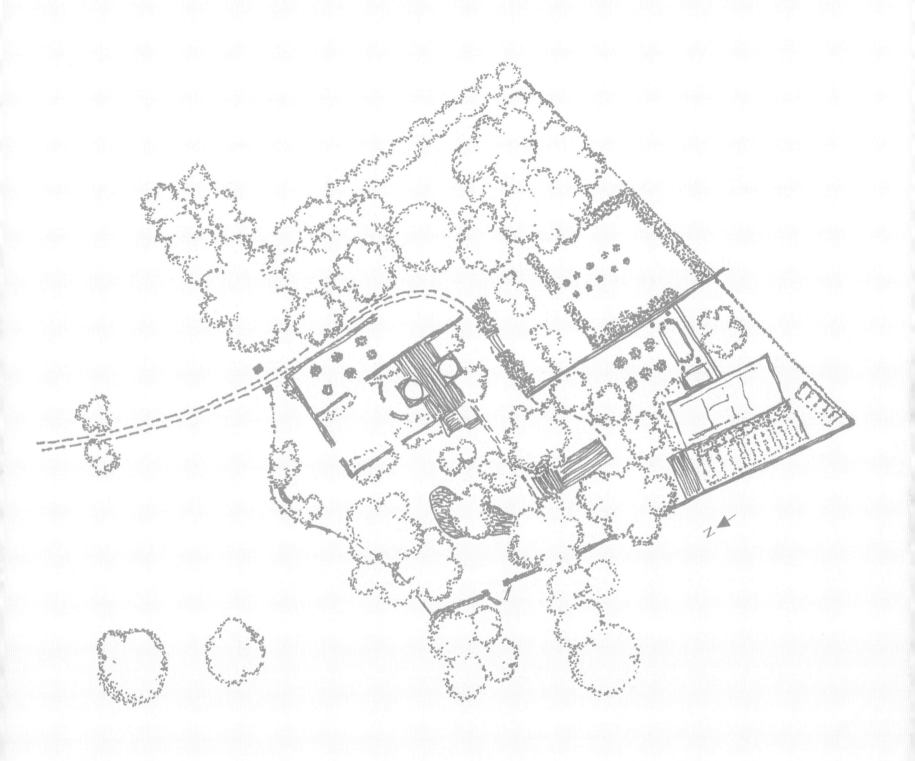

INGLENEUK

Sydney

I WILL OWN up to the fact that it is a difficult job designing a period style garden for a modern family, who require a house and garden that can accommodate the evolution of the family unit. Common requests from my clients include swimming pools, multiple car parking, lighting and even tennis courts. Finding the happy medium between function and aesthetics can be difficult.

The best approach to the situation is to start from a purely utilitarian point of view. A pool or a tennis court has a set size; a driveway or outdoor barbecue and dining area can't be too cramped. The set spaces can be arranged like a jigsaw puzzle and, once assembled in the most attractive and functional way, can be disguised by period aesthetics.

Ingleneuk is a perfect example of creating a modern house and garden disguised as an original work. Dating back to 1903, Ingleneuk is a Federation house built for a Mr Crossman. The house is large but not grand, and is situated on a rocky outcrop facing Sydney Harbour. Like many older homes in the district, it is built from timber, brick and stone. Some of the stone was even quarried on site for its construction, and has most likely been used to create the footings and lower skirt upon which the house sits. One of the most beautiful features of the house is the timberwork, the grand balconies, with intricate rails, posts and fascias providing the house with what I've always thought of as a bit of an oceanfront Hamptons' aesthetic. The high pitched tiled roof, weatherboard walls and quirky details such as the moon window on the upper floor balcony support my theory.

When my clients took over the property, they were faced with a challenge. Not only was the garden rundown but the house was also in need of major restoration works. Clive Lucas, arguably Sydney's most highly regarded heritage architect, was responsible for alterations to the house, bringing it in line with modern requirements but with a brief to maintain the heritage of the old home. This was the third time I would come across Clive Lucas on a job, and certainly not the last. He was integral to the renovation works at both Bronte House and Rona, and later we would also meet on works such as that at the 1835 John Verge mansion, Lyndhurst. My brief was similar to Clive's: to create a garden that incorporated the modern features a family requires, but was sympathetic to the period and architectural elements of the house.

Visiting the property for the first time in 2002, I was met with what was truly a derelict garden. None of the existing landscaping features was usable. Stone paths lay cracked and dangerous to walk on, walling had bowed or collapsed, and services had long reached their use-by date. But, being young and ready to take on a big project, I accepted the job of renovating the garden with the aim of creating one of the best properties in the district.

Part of the reason for its dilapidated state was that this was only the second time the house has changed hands since it had been built. This was both a good and a bad thing for the property. On the one hand, it meant that the garden layout was very close to its original format, but on the other, the original format did not work for the home in its current state. In addition, over the years, garden beds and plantings had been added in places where they may have done more harm than good, and the newer materials had no relevance whatsoever to the period. But the most interesting part of the landscape was that the house had been turned around.

When Ingleneuk was built, the entry was on its southern side, which is imposingly elevated above the surrounding landscape, and built with intricate timber detailing. Guests would alight from early motorised vehicles or carriages on the southern, lower side of the property, walk up 20 steps, along a path, then through an entry garden and lawn, up yet more steps, be impressed by the house and, providing they took the left-hand path rather than the right-hand one, end up at the portico of the formal entry. Thankfully, because of the popularity of the motor car and man's love of the shortcut, the entry to the property was now either by walking down the gently sloping path from the northern, high side of the property or by simply driving to the back door.

When Ingleneuk was built, the main entry to the house was on the harbour side of the property, shown here. In intervening years, and partly because of the popularity of the motor car, the entrance was switched to the higher, street side.

Reconfiguring the property so that it seemed as if the entry had always been from the high side was, however, a difficult task and required some radical changes. The existing tennis court was an immovable object and inspired the design of a long narrow perennial walk that ran down one side of it. Filled with a colour scheme of blue, silver and burgundy, the garden displays plenty of colour and flowers throughout the year.

The tennis court, although a blessing for property values, is a huge, immovable, flat green space, which uses vast amounts

Reconfiguring the property so that it seemed as if the entry had always been from the high side was a difficult task.

of potential entry garden. It was, however, a historic feature of the property and, with plantings of climbing roses and stephanotis on its boundary wires, became decorative as well. Working with utilitarian features such as tennis courts or parking areas is often a difficult task in landscaping. Many designers, often upon the request of clients, try to disguise or hide the feature behind a wall or hedge. This isn't always successful, though, and you will often find that working with a structure can lead to a more successful landscape. The tennis court fence here, for example, was made of timber and chicken wire rather than metal and heavy gauge mesh. The timber fence has a heritage feel and is more in keeping with the period of the house.

The formal entry to the property is through a dense perennial garden running the full length of the tennis court. The path is of sandstone flagging, a copy of the stone used

on the original entry path. The garden uses repeated stands of melianthus and phormium as key structural elements, while the more flowing parts of the garden are made from salvia, rosemary, teucrium and alternanthera. Clive Lucas added porticos placed at key locations on the path to provide a formal framework for the garden and enforce the idea that this is the main entry to the property.

A circular pond is the focal point of the end of the entry path and acts as a meeting place for visitors. From this one location, a guest can either enter the barbecue and tennis court area, proceed to the rear garden or enter the house. To make a successful new entry to the house, I had to redesign the old portico landing so that it could be approached from either side. The rear half of the landing was disassembled, a low wall was removed, and two new steps added in its place. The change worked well, as today it is impossible to tell it is a new feature.

The garden beyond the portico was designed to be easier to maintain than the entry garden. Designed primarily from buxus borders and transplanted camellias, the garden is simple yet elegant, with the main focus being seasonal aquatic plants in the pond.

As an interesting point, and being an unrelenting plantsman, I also added *Hedychium greenei* (scarlet ginger) behind the buxus hedges. It was an idea I had after seeing a photo of a buxus parterre filled with anthurium in a book on New Orleans gardens. Behind the camellia and buxus garden, I installed a collection of gardenias and hydrangeas, which was supported by transplanted *Magnolia* x *soulangeana.*

The entry path and those around the pond are constructed from sandstone crazy

LEFT TO RIGHT: inspired by a similarly unusual combination in a New Orleans garden, scarlet ginger has been planted behind the buxus hedges; a simple, rose-covered swing provides a romantic element in the garden.

LEFT TO RIGHT: the entry pond forms a hub from which guests can either enter the barbecue and tennis court area, proceed to the back garden or go into the house; the hydrangea is a key feature plant at Ingleneuk.

CLOCKWISE FROM LEFT: the arbour and new entry path with sandstone crazy paving and, clearly visible to the right, the timber and chicken wire tennis court fencing; swimming pool and pool house; the old entry path was relaid to accommodate the swimming pool.

paving. Specially selected to match the existing entry paving, the additional stonework provides a formal finish to the garden, making it appear more like the original main entry. Of course, the stonework now blends seamlessly into the slightly tweaked original southern side paths. Prior to my starting on the property, Clive Lucas had added a series of steps from the large deck on the rear of the house down to the garden. Unfortunately, the old stone paths didn't quite meet the new steps, and this provided me with the opportunity to redesign the entry path.

The harbour side garden of the house had only one redeeming feature – a Japanese box hedge that acted like a handrail to a lower stone retaining wall. The remaining garden was a mixture of overgrown shrubbery, weed species and lawn. Two *Cupressus torulosa* (Bhutan cypress) flanked the house, and to the western side was a mangy ginkgo and Norfolk Island hibiscus (one of the itchiest trees in horticulture). Although the trees in this part of the property weren't great, the additional structure they provided was sufficient to frame the house and provide a line between the different garden areas.

This part of the landscape, with its proximity to the large patio and veranda, was obviously going to be a key area for both entertaining and activities for the children. Because of this, I designed a colourful garden, utilising a combination of plants that I had used in both the entry and pond gardens.

Close to the house, in deep beds bordered by the new stone paths, is a combination of hydrangeas, buxus, gardenias and *Melianthus major*. On the western wall, I also planted feature *Melianthus major* and combined it with crinums, agapanthus, alternanthera, phormium and ornamental grasses. Two hedges of plumbago frame the garden, while a simple rose-covered swing provides a contrasting structure. In hindsight, I probably should have installed more evergreen screening material rather than ultra-exotics like melianthus – being close to the house, it's better not to be too seasonal, as it leaves nothing to admire in winter.

The lower, onetime entry garden at Ingleneuk houses an 11-metre (36-foot) swimming pool. Two positions were considered for the new pool, and the brief was that it be suitable for family use for the three small children and that it maintain the heritage of the Edwardian site. One suggested location was close to the tennis court, the other recreational feature of the property, and although this made perfect sense from a cultural point of view, it would have been very the keeping up with the Joneses mentality will see a flurry of similar pool designs that often don't reflect the accompanying architecture. This conundrum was faced with the design of Ingleneuk's pool.

A rectangular pool was designed and positioned parallel to the existing retaining walls. A spa was also installed in an alcove, divided from the pool by toughened glass, which was almost invisible. Inspired by one of the few private pools of the time, it was thought that the best look would be a painted finish and that the water line should be marked with oversized tiles similar to those found at an older public pool.

A problem was that, although painted pools were popular in the past, they are now not considered standard practice, and are not guaranteed by pool builders. Situations like this often come about when trying to follow

The brief for the new swimming pool was that it be suitable for the three children and maintain the heritage of the Edwardian site.

difficult to install because of the topography of the site.

A swimming pool area is a relatively new part of a landscape. It has only been in the past 70 years that the swimming pool proper has existed and, even then, it was more often than not in a commercial setting. The backyard swimming pool has spawned a following of landscapers and designers who have now become 'poolside specialists'. Innovations within that particular field of landscape design come swift and fast, and often it is design that bears the brunt of 'now' landscapes. New ideas are quickly posted, and heritage methods and you will find yourself resorting to the creation of bespoke finishes and products. In this case, along with a custom pool finish of a coloured fibreglass coating, came two brass pool filter lids, specially cast, plus sandstone coping.

Pool fencing, the design of which is limited by many rules and regulations, is now a requirement of most governments, and the thorn in the side of many landscape designers. The pool at Ingleneuk was no exception; at the rear of the property, the boundary fencing design was altered to double as a safety fence, and for the house side of the pool, a new steel palisade fence was designed, using 50 mm (2 inch) flat bar painted black. Dense garden plantings of *Viburnum odoratissimum* were then used as a hedge, growing through the fence and hiding its location.

The pool area reuses old stands of hydrangea against the existing stone wall as a foreground feature, while the opposite side of the garden has a row of *Magnolia grandiflora* 'Exmouth' with an underplanting of teucrium to provide a medium height dense planting for contrast. The magnolias are grown in an Italian-inspired pleached look, and tipped to prevent the trees from growing into the important harbour view.

The western end of the pool posed some issues. The fence by Clive Lucas was a lovely feature but too overpowering. The style of timberwork, like the house, had a very Hamptons' aesthetic, I felt, which inspired research into the works of the American design duo Oehme and van Sweden. Their use of ornamental grasses with Edwardian architecture had proved to be successful, and this led me to use *Miscanthus variegatus* as the main feature at the end of the pool.

Some of the simpler elements of a 'normal garden' become more difficult in a historic setting. The humble barbecue, a staple of any family yard, presents one of those issues. In the garden at Ingleneuk, a wood-fired barbecue, which doubles as a fireplace and stove, was required for the courtyard between the tennis court and kitchen. Bricks were sourced to match those on the house, and installing two stone slabs as benchtops created a period aesthetic. For the cooking surface, a bespoke firebox was created that could handle the higher temperatures created by wood fire, but still support standardised grills and cooktops.

A selection of house bricks and dark non-textured brick pavers to contrast with the feature sandstone was also sourced for the drive and formal entertaining areas of the design. Laid in a herringbone pattern with a header course, the paving is reasonably nondescript and provides much-needed contrast to the more decorative stonework.

Being able to maintain views over the surrounding district is a request most landscape designers face, and this project was no exception. The reconstruction of the large deck at the rear of the house and the framing of the view by taller trees gives the house the air of a maritime lookout. I have always envisaged an old brass telescope on the crow's nest-style top balcony. For the views alone, the garden needed to remain low, but still with enough height for interesting textures to be used in the foreground. This didn't mean that the property was devoid of trees, as there were plenty of locations for those, but clearly defined restrictions would need to be made on the garden design.

A request by the client for a vegetable garden and utility area was made late in the works. It was a good idea, as enough green waste was, by then, being produced to provide compost for the entire garden.

A large garden isn't all about just flowers and lawns; there is a dirty side to it. Materials, man-hours and money go into creating a great garden, and once the garden is complete – if there ever could be such a thing in a landscape – there is ongoing maintenance to consider. Period style gardens will often have more headaches and issues than their modern counterparts, but they are unique, and are for those people who want more out of the landscape than merely a green space.

A border, with its strong purple tones and mixed foliage, contains agapanthus, alternanthera, acanthus and gardenia, and reflects the burgundy of the house.

ROFFORD MANOR

Great Milton, Oxfordshire

ONE OF THE best designed new gardens I have ever been to is that at Rofford Manor. Designed by Michael Balston, it is a credit to both his work and that of the owners that such a harmonious existence can occur between an older house and a newer landscape.

I visited the garden of Rofford Manor on a mad dash to see as many Cotswolds gardens as I could in a day with my friend Penny, who told me that if I mentioned her in a book that I should say she is an extremely exciting and glamorous individual. This, of course, is all true but another of Penny's many talents is that she knows exactly who to ask and where to go to view the best gardens the English countryside has to offer. Incidentally, three gardens a day was the best we could do.

In a very private location, Rofford Manor leaves the casual passer-by with the thought 'that was a neat cluster of farmhouses'. With the gates closed, the garden at Rofford is nowhere to be seen, and the only difference between it and a cluster of farmhouses is the neatly mown lawn and trimmed edges on the roadside verge.

Mind you, I love working rural settings, where everything is done for a reason. Barns and sheds of a working property are designed for storing machinery or produce. A structure may be 10 metres (32 feet) long, not because it lines up with an opposing wall, but because that was the length of a plough or the size the farmer could afford to build at the time.

Rarely will the buildings have an aesthetic brick in them. Recycled or locally quarried stone are the building materials of choice: anything, as long as it's cheap. But what the buildings often lack in 'design' and much desired geometric placement, they make up for in character, charm and eclectic quirkiness.

The forecourt of Rofford is the hub that allows access to much of the property. Once an agricultural feature, the forecourt has been transformed into something more aesthetically pleasing without removing it from its original intentions. Around the court are the rear of the garden walls, the entry to the house, a barn and a stable with a dovecote. In typical utilitarian fashion, not all the buildings form a perfect rectangular shape, as many designers would desire. But the space works.

The stable is now a neat garaging space, with a gardener's toolshed attached to its side. The old barn at the end of the court has been transformed into an entertaining space. Both the garage and barn have essentially been modernised, but in a very tasteful, minimal way, which complements the original utilitarian design.

In order to achieve some symmetry in the garden and to provide a splash of green to the entry, a pleached lime tree hedge has been planted with a footing of English box. And, although not uniformly placed around the yard, it does manage to provide an overall feel of a symmetrical space.

The garden at Rofford Manor is a stunning mix of clipped formal hedges, mixed perennials and landscape design, with the house at the centre. On each side of the house, a different environment and feature has allowed the construction of a different garden room. With a similar use of materials, there is a great sense of continuity between the garden rooms, but each still has its own character.

I entered the garden from the forecourt via an elevated lily pond bordered by clipped buxus. The pond forms the centrepiece and is framed by the house and more pleached lime trees. When designing an older style pond, particularly for rural areas, I have often felt it needs to feel like a remnant of days gone by. An elevated pond with a solid coping can have the aesthetic of a trough or cistern, and give the impression of being reused as an ornamental feature. A similar approach can be taken with swimming pools and entertaining spaces.

This small box parterre opens up to a large expanse of level lawn. A new landform of the property, this expanse was created by the construction of a ha-ha wall, levelling the area from the reinvented barn at the end of the forecourt to a pergola nestled behind the house. The ha-ha has a slight elliptical curve, bending away from the house into the adjacent paddock. This curve is a very pretty feature but also provides more room than structured geometric platforms would. Designed as a way of creating a secure paddock without the need

View from one of the perennial borders towards the romantic Arts and Crafts-style courtyard at the rear of the nineteenth century farmhouse. Boston ivy creeps over the roof and chimney of the house.

LEFT TO RIGHT: the plant life attracts a variety of insects to the garden; a garden room alongside the swimming pool area, with a view of the pool house roof – mixed plantings of perennials and shrubs provide year-round presence, while obelisks provide structure.

for vista-destroying fencing, a ha-ha wall is as much a requirement in the landscape today as it was when first conceived. This ha-ha provides an uninterrupted view through to a lake at the bottom of the paddock. An even better feature, though, is that it provides a clean plinth-like structure for the house and garden when viewed from the lake.

It was impossible not to walk from the ha-ha to the lake. A small cottage folly rests on the far side, surrounded by reeds and willows. The lake is part of a small stream running through the property, and is one of two bodies of water side by side, the second of which is slightly upstream and feeds the main feature lake via a brick rill.

A structured rill is an easy yet effective way of providing interest with flowing water. By spacing the stepping of the levels, the water

> The rear of the house hides the more personal spaces in the garden. Within the walls and building elements is a very Arts and Crafts garden of stone flagging, perennials and romantic garden structures.

can be slowed or hastened, and made noisy or hardly audible. Instinctively, everyone enjoys the sight and sound of moving water.

The lakes are a masterful piece of aesthetic and engineering design. Water flows from a natural stream into the more hidden of the two; surrounded by bulrushes, this lake has a beautiful, natural appearance. The way it is viewed, lengthways rather than side-on, is unusual but makes it look bigger than it is. Simplicity is often the key to success, and the small rill proves that. The water flows playfully down small drops in the brickwork and into the main lake below. I have been responsible

for the construction of many lakes, and the edging treatments people choose have always fascinated me. On one side, the lake has a backdrop of natural reeds, while on the other, a contemporary gabion wall has been used. The end result is a line that lets the lawn end cleanly, a stable solution that prevents erosion.

Walking back to the garden proper from the paddock, you notice that the house and garden are very well proportioned. The landscape doesn't dominate the house, and nobody has pretended that the house is larger or more important than it is. Making too big a garden doesn't sound like a problem, but scale is relevant at both extremes and maintaining restraint is a key to good garden design.

The rear of the house hides the more personal spaces. Within the walls and building elements is a very Arts and Crafts garden of stone flagging, perennials and romantic garden structures, creating a small yet visually exciting court. Basic structure is the key to making such an intense garden. This garden is focused around stone flagging, which is then framed with timber obelisks, benches and potted clipped plants, the hard and clipped material contrasting with the lighter nature of the remaining loose foliage. The garden is also tied to some of the house elements, with doors and windows lining up with key elements of the landscape. There's nothing more special than the view from the house through to the croquet lawn and perennial borders.

Hedges of clipped yew form a garden room for the croquet lawn and are the backing for flanking perennial gardens. Key breaks have been left in the hedges to view the greater landscape. The central axis has a lovely vista through to an outer meadow and tree plantings of a grander Landscape garden style.

THIS PAGE: a stone-flagged courtyard close to the house, planted in Arts and Crafts style, with purple aster cascading over the benches, and pots of annuals. Following pages: pleached linden, with buxus footings, in the stable courtyard.

My favourite vista from this point is a small keyhole view through to the large pond and folly, seen through a gap on the southern side of the lawn. Again, a mixture of clipped and flowing shrubs and perennials fill the borders, providing shape and form up close as well as from a distance, from where they would more often be seen and appreciated.

The pool has been carefully installed in a private courtyard. Looking more like a pond than a swimming pool, the area, although modern, reflects all the grace of its surrounds. The paving stone is a heritage design flagstone and continues to the pool without the use of a coping. The pool tiles reflect the surrounding materials, with mottled white, blue and grey tiles providing an end colour in tune with its location. Choosing the right colours and materials for heritage pools is tough.

aligning with the southern axis. The low fence of the tennis court is the same height as the surrounding yew hedge and, although clearly visible, does not dominate in the landscape.

I have never fully appreciated the dedicated rose garden. They're time-consuming and, for a large portion of the year, not much to look at. It stems from my time in Sydney's Royal Botanic Gardens' rose garden, where my fortnightly job was to remove the spent flower heads and deadwood from over 600 plants. The task took three days and I was required to dip my secateurs into methylated spirits before cutting each plant. Rose gardens are, of course, sited in full sun and the job was hot, repetitive and painful. It did, however, give me time to think and, like every budding young rose gardener, I thought about how to make a better rose garden.

drawing you to investigate further, benches are romantically carved into buxus and no path is left unencumbered by a sprouting herb.

At Rofford, the varying walls and surfaces are an interesting feature. The brick and stone of the house are one element, with greenery another. Boston ivy, wisteria and roses are all grown as wall coverings. The wisteria is a particularly good feature as, rather than being a smothering plant, it can be trained to ramble.

A serious part of the landscape is the vegetable garden, a working space that's both functional and pleasing to the eye. The crops are in rows, as a production yard should be, and the garden is divided by brick paths. At the centre is an arbour covered in fruiting apples. Further frames and structures provide vertical accent to the often very low garden.

I've had the opportunity to design several vegetable gardens and, although it can seem a boring request, they can be as sophisticated as any other part of the landscape. The trick is to make them as well built and clean as possible. Hard masonry dividing paths, solid structures and uniform planting will provide rigidity for an often messy space.

> My favourite vista is a small keyhole view through to the large pond and folly, seen through a gap on the southern side of the lawn.

Standard materials often don't fit in with the surroundings, and I have found that, in more cases than not, something bespoke is required.

Although it is still a practical space, the addition of two large stone planters helps create a less pool-like environment and more of a garden. Potted plants also help tone down the pool as a one-off feature, as does disguising the pool-related amenities as existing farm outbuildings, covered in Boston ivy.

The tennis court is just as well hidden as the pool. The way this court has been approached has been to conceal the area in a space, created by the walls of the pool area and the hedges behind the main perennial garden

The rose garden at Rofford Manor is a better rose garden. Created in a garden room on the western side of the house, it is surrounded by a masonry wall and divided by flagstoned paths. This heavy reliance on stone in the garden maintains a drier microclimate with little humidity, allowing roses to thrive without pest and disease. The roses are repetitive groups of the same species, which is a little more contemporary than most, and I like the way the garden blends into the surrounding shrub and perennial landscape. This part of the garden is an adventure; low gateways have you wanting to discover what's beyond them. Hedges hide parts of the garden,

The vegetable garden at Rofford Manor is part of a whole that sums up exactly what period garden design is about. The entire garden is perfectly designed for modern use, with great spaces for entertaining and alfresco living. It is also a clean space with all areas having a sense of purpose. But the garden also reflects the style of the house, and complements, rather than contrasts with, the structures. Some areas have even been reinvented, but through clever design have retained their original aesthetic. The end result is a landscape that suits the architecture, while remaining very much a part of the present.

THIS PAGE, CLOCKWISE FROM LEFT: a random rubble wall beside the house; view of the ha-ha from the paddock; the main lake with estate fencing in the foreground. Following pages: the vegetable garden, showing the gardener's cottage to the right.

A mix of trees, including oaks, planes and maples, grows along the hellebore walk on the lower slopes of Moidart. The meandering pathway is scattered with sawdust, giving it a very unstructured feel.

MOIDART

Southern Highlands, New South Wales

EVERY YEAR I used to take a trip with my mother to the Southern Highlands town of Bowral. It's a short drive, about an hour and a half from Sydney but, importantly, involves a climate change that made the wealthy elite favour this particular region as a suitable landscape in which to create a summer retreat.

The boom in the district occurred predominantly in the early part of the twentieth century, coinciding with the Arts and Crafts and Art Deco movements. Fantastic houses and plenty of money encouraged the creation of equally fantastic gardens, and the climate, combined with rich mountain igneous soil, made the area suitable for growing varying Australian, European and Asiatic plants with relative ease.

Today, the area continues to develop in the thick of a revival that began in the late Eighties. Land, huge houses and larger gardens are again being developed in the area with a lot of enthusiasm. Requests for two to four hectare (five to ten acre) gardens have become common practice. At the time of writing, my own work in the Highlands was on four properties with a total of 22 hectares (55 acres) of landscaped parkland and garden proper.

The Southern Highlands is to Sydney what the Cotswolds is to London or the Hamptons to New York and, for designers and gardeners of those districts, it's a privilege to work in an area where the horticultural elite has sculpted the countryside.

Garden designing greats of the first half of the twentieth century included Edna Walling and Paul Sorensen, who had the enviable job of pioneering the way landscapes would and should be perceived for the new strains of architecture. Many of the great gardens of Australia have since appeared in the Southern Highlands and, like other great garden districts of the world, where one garden is created, others have followed.

As with European gardening, the seasons dictate when any particular element of landscaping takes place. Winters see frost and snow, with temperatures regularly below freezing, while in the summer months the Australian heat is still something to battle against, although the mean temperatures are lower than those outside the high country.

One garden of the district that has always inspired my works is Moidart and, although it is not a new garden created around existing architecture, it has continually been developed with a disregard for tradition but without losing its sense of purpose and thematic planning.

Constructed in the early 1930s for the Burns family, the house and garden have become the home of the Southern Highlands horticultural aesthetic and have been the hub of good taste for the past 70 years. Located in the heart of the Highlands in the well-to-do township of Burradoo, Moidart, like all gardens of its time, was designed to be a genteel retreat within a strongly agricultural aesthetic. The

house was designed by Laidley Dowling and positioned, typically, on the crest of a ridgeline with a view of the surrounding countryside.

A very formal house, Moidart uses varying architectural elements that make it difficult to place in a particular style. A symmetrical Georgian-inspired façade dominates, but with details hinting at Arts and Crafts. The southern veranda is fairly Australian colonial, but the colour and posts used have a slight Mediterranean feel. The rear of the house, however, reveals a strong Art Deco structure, with a stunning curved glass double-height window that lets light pour into the main foyer and grand staircase.

The garden was designed by a Mr Buckingham who, with the assistance of architect Laidley Dowling and Mr Shiress, a Burns family friend and amateur botanist, positioned all the trees and structural elements of the garden.

Like most landscapes of greater rural properties, the garden was created over a slope. This is never a problem, as the slope in a large garden ultimately provides the landscape with an interesting structure and designated points of change. Thematic design is possible, with each change in topography allowing a change in style or the introduction of a new feature. A terraced or sloping garden can even manage the use of water and irrigation more efficiently.

Of course, a terraced garden has its disadvantages. The cost of steps and walls is a problem as, too, are maintenance and access, but they shouldn't be things to complain about. Every garden needs some form of structural element. In a flat garden, the position of a wall or path is determined by the designer's skills with spatial awareness and proportion. A sloping garden practically designs itself, with stairs and walls placed where required, setting the framework for the planting.

The walls and the arrangement of the steps are very romantic in Moidart, and draw upon the garden's tendency to be Arts and Crafts inspired. Natural stone walls including ha-has provide the garden with a slight amount of structure without being overbearing. Australia's most famous gardener of the period was the Jekyll-inspired Edna Walling. Her designs frequently relied upon retaining walls to provide structure in the garden without dominating it. Her planting style was similar to that at Moidart and featured carefully positioned trees, organically set-out lawns and rambling low plantings and shrubs. The thinking behind it was that the garden, with its blend of colour and texture, takes on a more natural style.

As a horticulturalist, trees are very close to my heart and, as a designer, I appreciate and study the use and positioning of large scale plantings very closely. There is no other form of design in the world that needs to take into account such a changing dynamic. When creating a shrubbery or when working with perennials, the end result will not be vastly different in appearance from how the garden starts out, as most plants installed will grow at roughly the same rate, and aspects and conditions will remain similar throughout the life of the garden. When planting an arboretum or a large grove of trees, however,

the initial layout of the trees is very important, as the garden will not resemble the desired result for some time. This delay will not stop gardeners and owners wanting the rest of the garden planted. Obviously, a juvenile arboretum is a very open sunny space and requires a sun-tolerant garden to suit. However, over the following 10, 50 or even 100 years, the dynamic of that space changes. Branches create shadows, in turn creating cooler microclimates; large tree roots invade the soil, drawing moisture and nutrients away from lesser sized plants, and lower branches smother any hope of large understorey foliage growing tall.

Most gardens need to look great from day one and, at Moidart, initial intense planting was carried out. Although a horticulturalist may look at the planting today with contempt, as tree species are a little close together, it is all

The head gardener at Moidart told me that when the property was first planted, dynamite was used to break through the shale. Many of the trees in the garden were planted by a local, Clarrie Worner, who would apparently throw in a stick of dynamite and then 'run like hell'. Judging by the size of the trees, this method of planting was very successful and, although it sounds like fun, I'm not sure how Occupational Health and Safety would react if I were to continue the practice.

The sunken rose garden is one of the few major structural elements of the garden. Located on the southern side of the house and lying parallel to the wisteria-covered veranda, it appears to be an extension of the architecture. The design is slightly Arts and Crafts, with Art Deco details. Slivers of locally quarried stacked sandstone form the garden beds, while the paving is random sandstone

When the property was first planted, dynamite was used to break through the shale. Many of the trees in the garden were planted by a local, Clarrie Worner, who would apparently throw in a stick of dynamite and then 'run like hell'. Judging by the size of the trees, this method of planting, which sounds like fun, was very successful.

in hindsight and, in my opinion, the vision and foresight used to create such a beautiful setting of fantastic mature trees is extraordinary. The combination planting of an avenue of English planes (*Platanus* x *hybrida*) and deodars (*Cedrus deodara*) side by side down the drive to create a linking tunnel is very successful. The large green leaves of the platanus contrast with the fine blue-grey needles of the cedrus. The understorey planting of rhododendrons and maples adds another, more finely detailed layer to the picture.

flagging, both of which features were common in this period.

At the centre of the sunken garden is a crabapple, leaving the rest of the garden beds to be filled with mass plantings of roses and perennial ground covers. Further structure and contrast is provided by a large box hedge surrounding the garden. The additional greenery provided by the buxus tones down the heavy reliance on stone and offers a little coolness to the hot space. The reliance on stone actually gives a horticultural advantage

CLOCKWISE FROM TOP LEFT: a bluebell section of the lower walk; the main drive is lined with plane trees and deodar cedars; the copper beech on the south-east corner of the house; the lake and paddock at Moidart.

The vision and foresight used to create such a
beautiful setting of mature trees is extraordinary.

to the garden as, because of the high humidity, rose gardening in Australia is often a difficult task. The stone-surrounded rose gardens help create a microclimate that reduces the immediate humidity in the air, in turn reducing the frequency of fungal outbreaks and preventing pest and disease.

The sunken rose garden is a very impressive part of Moidart, and one that always gets a reaction from visitors – so much so that the success of a visit has, for a long time, been based upon the quality of the roses that week. To me, though, it's part of the garden that wows visitors too easily; the built nature of the garden and its delivery of the token horticultural plant, the rose, are classic crowd-pleasing gimmicks of the Arts and Crafts movement, and decoration for the sake of decoration. Realistically, the garden layout is a little cramped and stuffy; in my opinion, it should have taken a more simplified and classical approach.

The classical nature of the house entry and portico is reflected strongly in the immediate garden. Beds close to it have been thickly planted with *Hydrangea quercifolia* and may bush, and the central circular garden formally arranged with matching sentinel junipers and masses of iceberg roses. The display is fairly feminine, but suits the classical columns and doll's house aesthetic of the residence. The entry of the house faces east and takes advantage of a distant rural vista that runs from the centre of the front door. This view has cleverly been left open, but in an informal way, allowing keyhole glimpses of the surrounding countryside, so the viewer does not feel overwhelmed. Structurally, the formality of the house entry continues into the garden via the construction of stone garden

steps leading down to a lower terrace and, although this isn't a heavily built garden, the hint of further structure is enough to lead a visitor to believe that the structural, formal side of the landscape continues further from the house.

Not only known for its spectacular trees, Moidart is also home to some spectacular shaded bulb and perennial walks. Competition from roots of larger trees often makes it difficult to grow larger shrubbery plants. Below large trees, it's often much easier to grow smaller plants that only feed and draw moisture from the very top of the soil profile.

Moidart is a horticulturalist's garden. Along with the collection of mature trees in the greater garden, there is an extensive collection of smaller perennials, with some arranged in a trial and development garden. A dream to someone like me, it contains a mix of interesting perennials and shrubs. It's neatly placed within a clipped conifer room, and serves a dual purpose as a protected sunny lawn, accessed from the central part of the house. Within this space, Moidart is able to trial breed and grow new plant possibilities for the garden, and for the garden's commercial perennial nursery offshoot.

On the lower slopes of the garden at Moidart, hellebores and bluebells, which flower in succession, have been planted en masse either side of a path that snakes its way between the mature trees.

On the lower slopes of the garden at Moidart, hellebores and bluebells have been planted en masse either side of a path that snakes its way between the mature trees. The plantings flower in succession, with the hellebores blooming at the end of winter and bluebells flowering with the onset of spring. Mass plantings of bluebells, often in the form of a meadow, are a common occurrence in large rural gardens. But it's not often that hellebores are grown en masse and it surprises me that they are so effective. The deeply lobed, glossy leaves form a rough, flowing mass of green, and the soft purplish tones of the flowers add the right amount of interest to the landscape without being overbearing. In keeping with the Arts and Crafts feel, the garden is highly planted, and the meandering path of sawdust is also cute.

Business in large gardens forms a necessary evil. The cost of upkeep for larger estates and gardens runs into massive amounts of money per year, with the sad truth being that if the garden does not make a profit, it cannot exist.

I buy quite a few interesting odds and ends from Graham, the nursery operator and, incidentally, the head gardener at Moidart. Along with his knowledge of perennials and old English cattle, he has also given me advice on large scale gardens. He tells me that many of the plantings, whether they be suckering shrubs or ground-hugging perennials, can be maintained by mower, seasonally slashing the plants to the ground. Moidart's extensive collections of hostas, hellebores and other woodland perennials, as it happens, are perfectly suited to this.

PREVIOUS PAGES: a view under the copper beech close to the house, and showing a corner of the rose garden on the right. This page, left to right: a crabapple, surrounded by beds of roses and perennial ground covers, forms the central focus of the rose garden; one of Moidart's great attractions.

STONE FLAGGING

Stone flagging is a standard paving style in many Edwardian gardens. In the Arts and Crafts movement, the paving style digressed from the cleaner, simple Georgian format to more rustic designs such as crazy paving and complex pebble arrangements. In English gardens, the use of limestone was prevalent, while in Australia, sandstone was the material of choice. The garden at Ingleneuk contains sandstone crazy paving, matching the paving found on the original entry. Although this material is somewhat solid and rather expensive, many of the older gardens did not use particularly good construction methods, so you will often find these paths in need of repair.

FRAGRANCE

Gardenias, roses, murraya (orange jessamine) and other fragrant plants were very much a feature of Arts and Crafts gardens. The house, in a way, became an extension of the garden, and vice versa – plants were grown not just to look pretty outside but were also chosen for their suitability for picking and, if they had a nice scent, so much the better. The strange tapestry of colour in Arts and Crafts gardens continued into the house, with the use of wallpapers and floral fabrics. In the garden at Ingleneuk, *Gardenia augusta* 'Florida', a fairly new cultivar, is used extensively – it has many more flowers, denser foliage and more intense fragrance than the traditional gardenia.

PERENNIAL BORDER

The trickiest thing about a perennial border is creating controlled chaos rather than simply a mess. None of the plants need to be the same species; rather, it's important to work with forms. If the habit of the plant is to be short and squat, you can contrast that with something slightly different but then go back to a short and squat plant. The way to see if a bed is working is to unfocus the eyes slightly before you look at it – if you can't make out shapes and textures, it probably isn't that successful. Even while you're at the nursery choosing plants, arrange them in the trolley; if colours and textures don't look good there, they won't work in the garden.

EDWARDIAN (ARTS AND CRAFTS) GARDENS

GARDEN FURNITURE

Just as sculpture is difficult to choose for the garden, so, too, is picking the right garden furniture. It has to look good, but that's not enough – it has to be functional as well. For a family, for instance, an outdoor dining table has to seat a certain number of people and, while you may like the idea of single chairs, benches may be more practical. A lot of garden furniture is pretty boring, but if you do your research, you'll find some that both work and fit into the garden setting. Most people spend a lot of time choosing indoor furniture but then treat outdoor furniture as an afterthought, which is a shame, as it can make the difference between enjoying sitting outside and finding it horribly uncomfortable.

HYDRANGEA

The hydrangea is a staple plant of the Edwardian garden. Full blooming with lush green leaves and delicate detail, it longs to be cut and put in a vase. It's a plant, then, which can be used as a feature or backdrop outdoors and to provide decoration inside. The less sunny gardens of Ingleneuk contain a mixed planting of purple, burgundy and a little bit of pink, with the deep colour scheme designed to enhance the dark burgundy of the house. One of the great benefits of the hydrangea is that if you feel like a change of colour, a slight alteration of the pH level in the water will provide you with a completely different look.

PLANTS ON WALLS

Growing something on the wall is a great way of making the garden feel larger than it is. As you come across a vine-covered wall, the impression is of reaching a hedge rather than the terminal point of a garden. From a distance and with the wall lost in foliage, it feels as if the garden continues on. Plant something in front of that wall, and the wall acts as a backdrop, giving depth to the scene. You can't just plant anything – steer clear of creeping fig and English ivy, which both feed off the lime in the cement and end up damaging the wall. Boston ivy, with its season-changing foliage, is spectacular, and so too is creeping hydrangea, which snakes out across the wall and has masses of fragrant white flowers.

SPANISH MISSION GARDENS

An architectural style that's completely out of place in its adopted settings allows
an enormous amount of freedom in the garden.

THE SPANISH MISSION style is one of the oddities of the architectural world. It started out in California in the late nineteenth century, inspired by the highly romantic terracotta-roofed, whitewashed mission buildings left by the Spanish in California and Mexico. It gradually made its way to Australia and New Zealand, neither of which has any link whatsoever to Spain. There are a couple of reasons it became a popular style in the Antipodes in the first part of the twentieth century – for one thing, a lot of Australian architects turned to the United States for inspiration and liked what they saw; it almost wouldn't have mattered what that might have been. A few had worked there or in the Bahamas, where the style was also popular, and brought it back with them. And, after more than a century of building designs based on English models, it was thought that the Spanish Mission style was far more appropriate to Australia's largely Mediterranean climate.

As well as being a popular style for public buildings, Spanish, or Californian, Mission found its ways into the full range of houses, from suburban bungalows to grand mansions, one of the most spectacular of which is Boomerang, shown on the following pages. While there was a sliding scale of details, they did all share a few common features – rendered, textured walls in pastel colours, arches, spiral columns and posts, colonnaded walkways and, in the more elaborate versions, courtyards and cloisters.

Gardenwise, the best way to approach Spanish Mission is to go completely into the exotic – you can take it so far that it almost becomes grotesque but, for some reason, that's perfectly acceptable in this setting. A clam shell grotto doesn't look out of place in a Spanish Mission garden – in fact, it looks brilliant, which might be hard to believe. The same goes for plants – bold colours such as blue, purple and orange work wonderfully – there's no place here for subtlety. Succulents and palms look good here, instantly creating a sense of the exotic. One way to construct the garden is in groups, organised either by genus or by colour. If you were doing a blue garden, you could put agave and hydrangea alongside lilac and agapanthus, which sounds like a very strange mix but the blue colour ties it all together. Weird combinations are fine in a Spanish Mission garden, mainly because the idea of having a Spanish Mission house outside Spain is completely odd to start with. It gives you the freedom to go very slightly crazy.

Cloisters and courtyards, a standard element of Spanish design and found in some Spanish Mission gardens, are where you'd find plant material for culinary use and a water feature (which could be a fountain or pond); even here things could be a bit strange as well. You could plant very tall Abyssinian bananas with the much lower growing geranium, ginger or even roses – it sounds unlikely, but is a very typical Moorish pairing. You need to have structure in the garden – the banana trees provide a vertical accent, with the lower plantings forming balance around the base. Throughout the garden you'd repeat that vertical accent with lower plantings a number of times, and stay away from drifts of plants, found in earlier style gardens.

Pots, planted with anything from citrus or herbs to palms and succulents, are important in Spanish Mission gardens – the bold style of architecture, with its arches and colonnades, often lets you get away with oversized pots, sometimes more than a metre (3 feet) tall and in colour schemes to match the house.

Pattern is another vital element, and that can be found in the style of paving, used to create a Moorish symbol or, for instance, in the construction of a knot garden or parterre hedge, which can look perfect in this setting. In a modern version, you might create some of those patterns in a material like bluestone or basalt, or even concrete, or with a clipped Japanese box hedge – the effect will be quite traditional, although the materials may not necessarily be so.

The overall exoticism of Spanish Mission, from the architectural details of the house to the plants used in the garden, lends itself to dramatic lighting. Again, there's no room for subtlety here – uplighting and other quite theatrical effects can be used very effectively for emphasis.

In its most traditional form, the Spanish Mission garden is extremely high maintenance – for sheer logistical reasons you'd never attempt to build one on such a grand scale today. What you have to do is understand the thinking behind such gardens and use the key elements of colour, form and scale to construct a successful and far less labour-intensive modern version.

A mosaic pond in the centre of the cloister at Boomerang, an opulent Spanish Mission house in Sydney. The garden is planted with an exotic mix including, as shown, the fan-like succulent *Aloe plicatilis*.

BOOMERANG

Elizabeth Bay, Sydney

DURING THE EARLY part of the twentieth century, a completely new style of architecture, Spanish Mission, reached Australia. As Spanish Mission revival architecture developed over the years and across the continents, it became more and more elaborate, as it looked towards the Moorish region of southern Spain for inspiration. Courtyards, cloisters, colourful tiles, arched colonnades, terracotta-tiled roofs and decorative towers all became features of the architectural style. Probably the best example of Spanish Mission architecture in Australia is Boomerang, one of my favourite houses, and the gardens of which I have designed. Located on Sydney Harbour, it was built in the 1920s, with picturesque views looking north to the shipping lane. The house combines a look of hedonistic prosperity with exotic traditional styling and has remained generally untouched over the years.

In the mansion suburb of Elizabeth Bay and built for the Albert family of sheet music fame, Boomerang was to be the best house in the city. The most expensive house built at the time, it originally sat on a little under a hectare (2.5 acres) of land with the built elements of the massive home sprawling over a quarter of that space. The Alberts' use of it was, however, fairly chequered, with much of the family focusing on ventures other than that of residing in and developing Boomerang. Interest in the property waned over the years, to the extent that during the Seventies no one lived in it. This, initially, had little effect on the house, as rendered bricks, stone and tiles require little or no upkeep. The garden, however, was not so lucky.

It became rundown, with no thought given to direction, development of design or maintenance of external materials. With the garden at the end of its lifespan, the house, which by this time was deteriorating, was sold. A renovator's and developer's delight, the huge property was perfect for anyone willing to make a quick buck by subdividing. Millions were made in the selling-off of the tennis court and associated park-like garden which, although it represented a fair chunk of the property, is rarely missed as it was an annexe hidden by neighbouring buildings.

Strangely enough, with all the time and planning that had gone into the garden, the original tennis court ran east–west instead of the required north–south, even though the space was available. The Alberts were obviously not a sporting family.

The original garden designer for Boomerang, Max Shelley, would have been turning in his grave, for one result of the sale was that his designed layout for all of the harbourside gardens would be destroyed, never to be replaced.

The sale of Boomerang after the occupation of the Alberts was, for a while, the beginning of the end for the house and garden. The property had a succession of short-term owners, almost all determined to own a trophy house but not to turn it into a home. It was regularly hired out as a location, as successive owners tried to spin a dollar from it, while sitting out their time waiting for property prices to rise. Without doubt, Boomerang's most famous, international moment was its appearance in Tom Cruise's *Mission Impossible II*, which included shots of the driveway entry and renovated guesthouse bathroom.

My own part in the Boomerang saga began with a phone call from the Schaeffers, who requested my team remove hebes and society garlic from the terrace troughs and replace them with something more suitable. The double-height trough on the terrace reminded me of ones in the San Francisco garden Filoli, but rather than using buxus, I planted two rows of gardenias to be clipped as a double-height hedge.

When I started, I walked through the property in shock. How could such a grand house and garden get so dilapidated? Basic horticulture was rotting under dead limbs and mountains of non-biodegradable pine bark mulch. I finished my job for the Schaeffers and they gave me a couple of days to smarten up the garden before a function. It would take a lot more than that to resurrect the home.

In 2005, the house was bought by transport magnate Lindsay Fox and his wife, Paula. Paula was good friends with my previous employer, Leo Schofield, and I was

The sunken garden in the forecourt of Boomerang. On the street side of the property, the garden has been designed with a composite planting of low maintenance plants, including buxus, teucrium and *Agave attenuata*.

PREVIOUS PAGES: the view from the portico and across the sunken garden towards the street, showing the two *Phoenix canariensis* planted to screen neighbouring apartment buildings. This page: the cloister garden, towards the harbourside garden.

asked if I was interested in redesigning and constructing the garden. I didn't hesitate for a minute before accepting.

The Foxes are a Melbourne-based family who saw a need for a Sydney residence. Known for their generosity towards public gardens, the Foxes were just what Boomerang required – stability. The constant changing of hands with no long-term goal meant that structural efforts to improve the property would never be made and only superficial attempts to improve it would take place.

When I took over the garden, its state of dilapidation was stable but, overall, it was far removed from the designer's original intentions. The harbourside flagstoned paths that had been removed to construct a pool were now used to fill almost all planting space in a Moorish cloister garden on the western side of the house. All the gardens had extensive weed infestations, and incorrect arboriculture and pruning methods had left many of the trees in very poor health. Clearly, there was a lot of work to be done.

All gardens between the street and house were in critical need of renovation, with the soil being the first challenge. When a property either sits dormant or has a high turnover of owners, basic horticulture is forgotten. Using the rule 'Your garden is only as good as its soil', it was decided that all the soil in Boomerang's gardens would be replaced, and deep cultivation would be needed to reinvigorate garden life. This was a difficult task as large trees had a mass of roots in the old soil, and years of redirected or obsolete services would need to be removed or replaced. The *Cupressus torulosa* (Bhutan cypress) conifers that line the sunken garden proved to be a particular issue as roots plus years of dropped foliage had turned the soil arid and acidic.

In other areas of the garden, a build-up of weeds and perennials needed to be removed before work on the soil could begin. In some cases, weed species had actually turned into trees. An African olive on the western side of the drive was large enough to warrant council permission for its removal. In the guesthouse garden, great care needed to be taken around a mango and an avocado. Both trees were rumoured to have been planted in the 1930s, making them some of the oldest trees in the district, and certainly the oldest fruiting trees in the region. There's a story that the trees were part of the original settler's orchard, which would have them planted in the 1830s. It's doubtful but, nonetheless, a lovely thought.

Ten tip trucks of root-infested pine bark-laden dead soil eventually left the street side garden of Boomerang, leaving me with a compacted, sandy, hydrophobic wasteland. Compost and decomposed organic material are universally the best soil conditioners for an older garden, and had to be turned into the soil to a depth of 300mm (1 foot).

A garden design was not actually drafted for Boomerang until I was left with a completely clean slate. The brief from the client was to restore as much as possible and to create a garden in keeping with the house. Some original photographs from old *House and Garden* and *Home Beautiful* magazines were available, as too was an article entitled 'The Remarkable Mr Shelley', about the designer of the garden, written by a member of the Historic Council.

After studying the photographs from the 1930s and researching other significant properties with similar architecture, it was decided that the garden would be simplified around the high-traffic areas, making it easier to maintain. Some of the influences were the Alhambra in Spain, Ganna Walska's amazing Lotusland in California and the works of Spain's premier contemporary landscape architect, Fernando Caruncho.

The ideas from the Alhambra and Lotusland provided me with the inspiration to be creative with bold planting schemes, while the works of Caruncho reinforced the ideas that the garden be functional and that the planting of off-the-wall elements is best applied merely to sections of the landscape rather than becoming the entire landscape itself. The result is that all the gardens vary, with the sunken central garden designed

When I took over the garden, its state of dilapidation was stable but, overall, it was far removed from the designer's original intentions.

from a composite planting of simple buxus, teucrium and *Agave attenuata*, plants that are horticulturally desirable and low maintenance.

The guesthouse garden, now the blue garden, was filled with as much blue as possible, and the western garden became a mass of subtropical foliage.

Boomerang is entered from a narrow one-way street through either large vehicular gates or a small pedestrian one, delivering you to the heart of the sunken central garden.

PREVIOUS PAGES, LEFT TO RIGHT: the gate leading to the now-removed tennis court; tiles bordering the portico; wall fountain and pond in the entry. This page: the formal terrace on the harbour side of the garden – hedges of gardenia and buxus are clearly visible.

An axis runs from the front gate, through the house to the harbour. Boomerang is often known as the peacock house, and avian motifs are subtly located down this line, on the front gate ironwork and dividing the rooms through the centre of the house.

Lined with *Cupressus torulosa* and focused around a central pond, the sunken garden is classically Spanish. Paths run either side of the pond to the front portico, via a second pond made from mosaic tiles and four plantings of trachycarpus palms. Buxus and *Trachelospermum jasminoides* (star jasmine) have been used under the cupressus as a double hedge, which is contrasted by clipped balls of teucrium and giant stands of *Agave attenuata*. Looking from the portico to the sunken garden, two *Phoenix canariensis* (Canary Island date palm) dominate the landscape, providing a backdrop and much

To the west of the sunken garden is a rambling garden made up of drifts of ginger, clivia and hibiscus. An old *Camellia japonica* also provides some shade for tree ferns, bird's nest ferns and monstera.

All of the gardens on the street side of the house have highly built elements to support them. Heavy rendered walls in a subtle peach colour frame the drive and the property. The drive and paths provide quite a contrast, with their highly detailed brick paving using three colours of brick, raked out mortar lines, a header course and an angled border. It all sounds a little over the top but, really, it suits the flamboyant architecture perfectly.

The blue door to the garage at the end of the courtyard was my inspiration for the blue garden, as was the surrounding architecture. In original photos, the garden was actually a bit kitsch and drew nothing from the

the centre was a three-tiered fountain with spouting Cupid. Again, the garden missed the point, but at least it was a step in the right direction and easily salvageable to become a thing of beauty.

Many designers forget that when working with striking architecture, particularly period architecture, you should step away from your personal tastes and rely upon proven design associations from history, or the house itself, to complete the design. In Boomerang's case, a bold colour scheme and gaudy arrangements suit the property perfectly.

Boomerang is the first property I have worked on with a cloister garden. A cloister is basically a covered open breezeway that forms a courtyard. Boomerang's cloister is on the western side of the house and its courtyard is a densely gardened space, laid out in a Moorish tapestry of stone and gardens.

The Alberts originally had many of the intricate gardens planted with giant ensete bananas, roses and flowering perennials. The perennials worked well but the roses were a problem because of the lack of air flow, and the giant bananas seemed like a good idea but became too unruly for the small garden.

When I arrived, the cloister gardens had been all but removed, infilled with stone plundered from the destroyed harbourside garden. All that remained were eight small beds of palms and bay. The stone infilling was easy to remove and the reinstatement of the original pattern was possible.

After reading of the failures of Shelley's original plantings, I changed the colour scheme of the garden and set it out relying upon the surrounding roof tiles as a colour palette. Yellow gazanias, hemerocallis and lemons; orange nasturtium and aloes; and blue

The harbourside garden at Boomerang is the one part of the property that bears least resemblance to its original layout or intent.

needed height to the arrangement. These trees were brought in to obscure neighbouring apartment buildings, which overlooked the entry garden and became the focal point of the view from the house. It was a simple solution, but some may have questioned it when I suggested it, as the trees were not an original feature of the property.

To the east of the sunken garden is the garage, with guesthouse above, and a courtyard of sandstone pavers and mini mondo grass, strongly supported by lashings of blue. Blue hydrangeas fill the surrounding gardens, and a collection of giant blue glazed pots focus on a blue door at the end of the yard.

surrounding structure. A mock wishing well was constructed in the centre of a lawn, surrounded by sandstone garden coping protecting a collection of marigolds and fuchsias. Stepping stones led would-be luck seekers to the well and on to the guesthouse.

How this garden came about, I'm not quite sure, but I'm glad it no longer exists. Its replacement was, however, also a reflection of its time, circa 1988, on the cutting edge of the white and green garden boom. That garden was then transformed into a reasonably formal space of regular sandstone flagging, bordered with mini mondo grass and narrow gardens behind retaining walls. Replacing the well in

echium, salvia and teucrium make up the new colour scheme – finally, one with relevance to the house. In any environment, setting a thematic plan is often the best way to limit your plant selection and to create a colour palette that suits the design.

The harbourside garden at Boomerang is the one part of the property that bears least resemblance to its original layout or intent. And although that may sound like a bit of a disadvantage, it couldn't be better.

Shelley's original layout for the harbour garden was of two concentric circular perennial gardens bisected by two open flagstone paths. I've always thought this was an unusual detail, as the perennial garden had more of an English design that didn't quite suit the overall theme of the property. Whether or not this was Shelley's intention or came about as the result of requests from the owners is not known, but its design does fit in with much of Shelley's other work in more traditionally styled properties.

The original design seemed too busy, so when the property changed hands in the late Seventies and the new owner removed the garden and replaced it with a large swimming pool, I could see what he was up to. The pool installed in the 1980s had a design somewhat in keeping with the property and it does have a mosaic tile 'Boomerang' logo installed on its floor. But it was the owner's need to highlight his initials within the word 'BooMeRang' that is a wonder to many. I actually like the fact that the owner was so brazen – in a house of this stature, there is a need for controversy in a playboy kind of a way.

From the terrace looking to the harbour, the now thickly hedged gardenias I installed for the Schaeffers have simplified the area and set the standard for the rest of the property. Thick, clipped hedges and dense perennials fill deep gardens, with the idea of providing solid texture from distant internal views and screening from prying eyes. Many of the plants used in the three streetfront gardens come together in the harbourside garden. Elephant's ears and agapanthus fill many of the perennial gardens, and teucrium is used as a hedge rather than as balls to punctuate the end of the lawn.

After consultation with the Foxes it was decided that the pool would remain a feature and, because of its prominent position, would have an impact on the design of the surrounding gardens, all of which would be set equidistant from the pool's edge. Large tree plantings of phoenix palms, jacaranda and oleander have begun to fill the flanking garden beds, providing privacy and depth where once the extent of the garden would have sufficed.

You don't always get your way with jobs, and even with the amount of work achieved at Boomerang, I still have a small dream for a Moorish rill and a La Mortella-inspired path as my own little pièce de résistance. But good things may have to wait.

What I learnt from Boomerang is that not only does the dynamic of a garden need to be observed but the surrounding influences of a community and recent development can have a major impact on the decision making in a heritage property. Council rules and regulations and a community's heartfelt ownership over a heritage property often need to be addressed. You need also to be selective about what is important to the site. Did the original design intent work for that property or was it flawed from the beginning? Just because a garden is old, I've realised, doesn't necessarily mean that it is good.

The cloister, from the harbourside garden and looking out towards the street. Replanted in recent years, the garden takes its colour cue from the surrounding roof tiles.

DIRT AND SOOT

A rustic patina will only be acceptable if, when you touch the aged surface, dirt and grime do not come off on your hands. No one could remember if the walls at Boomerang had ever been cleaned, but when they received a scrub at the beginning of works, everyone was amazed. Years of city smog and soot had deposited a brown layer over the walls, thick enough to mask the true colour of the property. The job took more than four weeks to complete, and required the purchase of a second cleaning machine after the first one died from fatigue.

GROTESQUE

Spanish Mission is one of the few design styles that challenges the boundaries of taste. The architecture itself is, in all honesty, an acquired taste and how you treat it can be equally confronting. Typically, the furniture for many of these houses needs to be big and bold and, although the colour scheme may be pale overall, there should always be a redeeming feature which makes the furniture stand out in the arrangement. Outdoor objects and pots also need to adopt similar features.

GREY

Spanish garden design provides the opportunity to display colour on both ends of the scale. Loud and proud is the design trait of many modern Spanish-inspired gardens, with bougainvillea, geranium and oleander the plants of choice. True Spanish design is, however, more sophisticated, and includes more subtle tones and textures. The main gardens at Boomerang have an overall colouring of greys and greens, made from low hedges and clumped feature plants. The front sunken garden is a combination of clipped teucrium balls, buxus hedging and *Agave attenuata*, while the harbourside garden uses teucrium as a hedge, flanked by white flowering Indian hawthorn, clipped into a low cloud shape.

in detail
SPANISH MISSION GARDENS

TERRACES

At its best, a garden terrace adjacent to a house is an extension of the house itself. It needs to be on the same level to be truly successful, and deep enough to be a useful space. Opening off the sunroom and also accessible from the dining and drawing rooms, the terrace at Boomerang has proven to be one of the garden's most regularly used assets. In warmer regions of the world, the terrace may be even more useful than the enclosed rooms of the house. Sydney's temperate climate and the harbour view make this part of the garden a seasonal success.

CLOISTER

A cloister is a roofed breezeway surrounding a courtyard. A common design feature of Moorish architecture, it allows a person to get from one point to another without being in the elements while, at the same time enjoying the cooling environment of an open-air landscape. The courtyard in the centre of a cloister is often used as a space for relaxation or as a hub for scented and culinary plants. The cloister at Boomerang combines the traits of a relaxation garden with those of a focused edible yard. The soothing sounds of running water are complemented by scented geranium and flowering plants, while lemon trees, nasturtiums and clipped rosemary are great additions to the kitchen.

PAVING

The Moorish inspired patterns of a Spanish Mission style garden are often evident in the paving. The original gardens of Spain used brick, pebbles, stone and tiles, often in combination. In the garden of Boomerang, the simple utilitarian structure of a driveway, like the terrace, has been turned into a work of art with the arrangement of an intricate brick pattern. Laid on concrete, the body of the work is a herringbone pattern in which each brick has been individually set on its side and set apart with a mortar joint, while the borders are laid in a stretcher bond pattern, bullet pointed with brick ends. The real detail, however, comes from the indented mortar joints, which look impressive but are difficult to keep clean.

HOMESTEAD GARDENS

Often developing spontaneously as a response to an unfamiliar environment,
homestead gardens represent gardening in its truest form.

OF ALL THE types of garden that exist around the world, colonial and Australian homestead gardens, more than any other, are ones that have developed spontaneously. Whether you're considering, at one end of the spectrum, gardens in the arid Australian bush or, at the other, those in lush regions of the West Indies and Indonesia, these are gardens that have never been designed but, instead, have evolved organically over time and often as a way of bringing a small touch of domesticity and normality into an alien environment.

Consider the history around most of these gardens, which started out as subsistence farms as settlers moved into an area to begin a new life. Trees were planted not for ornament but for their fruit or for crops, and so you'll find date palms, coconut trees, rubber trees, mangoes and the like creeping from the plantation into an area near the house. The garden, as such, came about as a last priority, and only if there was a bit of money left after all other expenses were taken care of.

It's no coincidence that those early gardens were generally started by the women of the house, often as an antidote to boredom, with their husbands away or working long hours, and to create a reminder of their homeland. Those gardens, which sometimes have a feminine twist, developed in a haphazard way – around a tree, to start with, or fanning out from the house, only as far as was manageable at the time, but growing as resources became available. Climbing roses and other creepers were often planted against veranda posts in an attempt to make the house look prettier than it was. Even today, climbers can enhance an appealing country house even further and instantly give a period feel.

Colonial gardens had no precedents – French, English, Spanish or Dutch settlers brought a few cultural impressions from home, and tried to integrate them but, on the whole, these gardens were freer than anything found elsewhere. A thing most have in common is that they developed through trial and error: coming from temperate climates to either highly arid or lush tropical environments, gardeners had no idea what they were doing. Error was par for the course in these confronting environments; not only were the plants different from anything the settlers had ever seen, there were also often wild animals lurking in the bushes. Whatever managed to survive became part of the landscape, and gardening could be a hazardous business.

This is gardening at its truest – the garden was created not to impress anyone but purely for the passion of gardening, as a means of escape or as a way of making sense of life. On a practical level, one aspect of the garden in Australia, the sentry planting of a pair of tall trees at the entrance to the house, positions the property in the landscape, acting as a landmark for visitors. This is something that, even today, can be re-created effectively. Suitable trees for Australian conditions would be *Araucaria bidwillii* (bunya pine) or *Araucaria cunninghamii* (hoop pine). Early coastal settlers used a similar method when they planted *Araucaria heterophylla* (Norfolk Island pine) near the house, hoping, usually unsuccessfully, that the tall trees would act as beacons for passing ships. They also believed, wrongly, the timber would be good for masts.

Plants used in colonial gardens of the West Indies were often those found on the journey from Europe, so they include poinciana and palms, which were considered exotic. In any colonial or Australian homestead garden, use should be made of native flora, both as a way of creating a sense of place and also, practically, to help ensure that the garden will grow. The early settlers often viewed native flora as if it were something far more familiar; you only have to look, for instance, at the idealised Australian landscape paintings by early nineteenth century artists to discover that they were depicting what they wanted to see – European plants and trees – rather than what was in front of their eyes. Now, we should embrace that same native flora and use it in key areas, such as at the entrance to the property, as is the case of Cruden Farm's eucalypt drive (page 190), which has an understorey of open grassy paddock rather than scrub and bush. Surrounding fences are of Australian hardwood and the driveway itself is of sandstone crush, all particularly appropriate for the location.

While early colonial gardeners had little to work with in the way of plant material and everything against them in terms of developing a garden, life is much easier these days. The main thing to consider with a colonial or homestead garden is the importance of a sense of place, however you may want to evoke that, and to completely ignore the idea of rules – in this case, they just don't apply.

A view towards the old entry of part of the original house at Cruden Farm in Victoria, a property owned by Dame Elisabeth Murdoch since the 1920s. In the dynamic and constantly evolving garden, an oak tree stands among a drift of plectranthus.

CRUDEN FARM
Langwarrin, Victoria

CRUDEN FARM IS Australia's forever evolving heritage garden and the result of the passion of one person, Dame Elisabeth Murdoch. Not content to rest on her laurels, she has been continuously developing the garden, with the experience that comes from maturity and the energy that only comes from a gardener.

When I first visited, I wasn't sure what to expect. The only photos I had seen were of the gum-lined driveway, with a quote from David Hicks saying it was one of the most beautiful he had seen. Coming from a man I'd thought had seen it all, this was a huge statement and warranted further exploration.

Was it just that as an Australian I didn't believe that the common gum tree could create that great an avenue, or was it that Hicks saw it as something exotic compared with his Cotswolds home? Whatever the answer, I couldn't wait to see the drive for myself.

I had previously met Dame Elisabeth when she came to visit Bronte House, and although she was unable to view the whole garden because of its many steep steps, her approval of the work she did see meant a lot to me. Luckily for me on my first visit to Cruden Farm, she had a small window of time, between breakfast with friends and a charity event, in which I could see the garden.

David Hicks was right: the drive is something to behold. What's more, it shows incredible forward thinking on Dame Elisabeth's part to use gums in its design – only recently have the majority of the gardening community come to understand that Australian natives could be used in such a manner. Lemon scented gums (once referred to as *Eucalyptus citriodora* but now botanically known as *Corymbia citriodora*) display a mottled bark that changes colour with the varying light of the day. Each tree is evenly spaced; however the natural twists and informal growth of the species break any notion of formality, the design aesthetic paying homage to the unique Australian bush. In a strange contrast, wild gladioli spring up at the base of the trees, adding yet another dynamic to an already spectacular drive.

The acceptance of a eucalypt tree as a suitable ornamental is further stressed in the garden with individual specimen plantings. Some people may not like the trees as features, especially against a backdrop of European plantings. I, however, love the contrast between the plant types, the rambling habit, smoky green leaves and flaky bark, which are all features not found in exotic plantings.

The main drive continues right up to the front door of Cruden Farm. This part of the house seems rather odd, especially when one has a peek at its northern and southern sides, which reveal the quaint building it once was.

In 1929, Elisabeth and her husband, Keith, went overseas. As they were going to be away for a long time, Keith felt it was the perfect chance to renovate. Before leaving, he approved a plan, and work was expected to be completed before their return. Building was the same then as it is today, and when they got back the house was unfinished, over budget and not to Elisabeth's liking.

It was too square and imposing, a blight upon the landscape, according to Elisabeth, who made her disapproval felt, leading to a new design decision. At Keith's suggestion, they employed up-and-coming garden designer and writer Edna Walling. Edna's style had been influenced by that of the great English designer Gertrude Jekyll, as is evident in the perennial borders she created and the structural elements she designed. Although Edna's stance in the landscape is almost masculine, which I can imagine was required when dealing with the macho world of landscape contractors, her designs are distinctly feminine.

For Cruden Farm, Edna designed two walled rooms, a series of low freestanding walls and a gate separating the southern garden from the forecourt to the house. The walled gardens were the supposed focal points and, although not particularly liked by Dame Elisabeth, they have become a famed part of the property.

In my opinion, Dame Elisabeth was quite right not to admire their construction. The

Some people may not like eucalypts as features, especially against a backdrop of European plantings. I, however, love the contrast between the plant types, the rambling habit, smoky green leaves and flaky bark.

rooms are very small, which is both an aesthetic and environmental problem. She has said that the second rose garden room was never suited to roses as the walls prevented air flow during the day and in the afternoon created too much heat, which scalded the plants.

The walled gardens have remained a feature, and are now regarded as an important piece of the garden's history. Although not always well received, they are one of the best examples of 1930s Australian garden style.

On the northern side of the house, the remnants of the original rambling rural cottage that Dame Elisabeth loved when

PREVIOUS PAGES: the eucalyptus-lined driveway, with gladioli between the gums, was once described by David Hicks as one of the most beautiful he had seen. Opposite page: looking towards the entry to the new garden, with plectranthus in the foreground.

LEFT TO RIGHT: the 1920s extension to the house has distinctive echoes of the American Deep South – the low stone wall is part of Edna Walling's design; head gardener Michael Morrison at work in the forecourt of the rambling stone stable, which can be seen in the background.

CRUDEN FARM IS Australia's forever evolving heritage garden and the result of the passion of one person, Dame Elisabeth Murdoch. Not content to rest on her laurels, she has been continuously developing the garden, with the experience that comes from maturity and the energy that only comes from a gardener.

When I first visited, I wasn't sure what to expect. The only photos I had seen were of the gum-lined driveway, with a quote from David Hicks saying it was one of the most beautiful he had seen. Coming from a man I'd thought had seen it all, this was a huge statement and warranted further exploration.

Was it just that as an Australian I didn't believe that the common gum tree could create that great an avenue, or was it that Hicks saw it as something exotic compared with his Cotswolds home? Whatever the answer, I couldn't wait to see the drive for myself.

I had previously met Dame Elisabeth when she came to visit Bronte House, and although she was unable to view the whole garden because of its many steep steps, her approval of the work she did see meant a lot to me. Luckily for me on my first visit to Cruden Farm, she had a small window of time, between breakfast with friends and a charity event, in which I could see the garden.

David Hicks was right: the drive is something to behold. What's more, it shows incredible forward thinking on Dame Elisabeth's part to use gums in its design – only recently have the majority of the gardening community come to understand that Australian natives could be used in such a manner. Lemon scented gums (once referred to as *Eucalyptus citriodora* but now botanically known as *Corymbia citriodora*) display a mottled bark that changes colour

TOP: view over the utilitarian stable gate towards the house and Dame Elisabeth's rose garden.
Below: the Boston-ivy-covered entry to Edna Walling's walled garden, with a bronze brolga guarding the gateway.

stick to one thematic plan in a property. It is important, though, for the transition from one theme to another to relate to the overall design. In the case of Cruden Farm, the dominating feature is the layout and positioning of feature specimen trees. The trees provide the garden and structures with a perfect backdrop, or have themselves become focal points around which gardens have been created. Dame Elisabeth's forward thinking also meant that the species of trees would be vast and interesting, leaving a seamless blend of exotics and natives, resulting in a unique garden.

One framed view that left me amazed is that from the house to the stable and vice versa. In the shade of the dominating elm trees, you catch a glimpse of a *Eucalyptus maculata* and the paddock stone wall of the stable. The overall feeling is of a truly iconic view of rural Australian landscape design.

Strangely, though, the reverse view will have you believing you're on a cotton farm in the Deep South. The tall timber columns of the house, looking very American plantation against the brilliant green of the dense elms, send a completely misleading message about where you are and what hemisphere you're in.

The stable and its surrounding gardens are an interesting feature of Cruden Farm. The stone gardens of Edna Walling were constructed before the stable, which is hard to believe as they feel as if they had been built around the structure, and would have looked very unusual without the stable.

The success of the stable, in my mind, can be attributed to the way in which good siting of landscape features and an understanding of restraint can produce good architecture. The stable is neither too big nor too small. Its rambling layout provides the area with enough

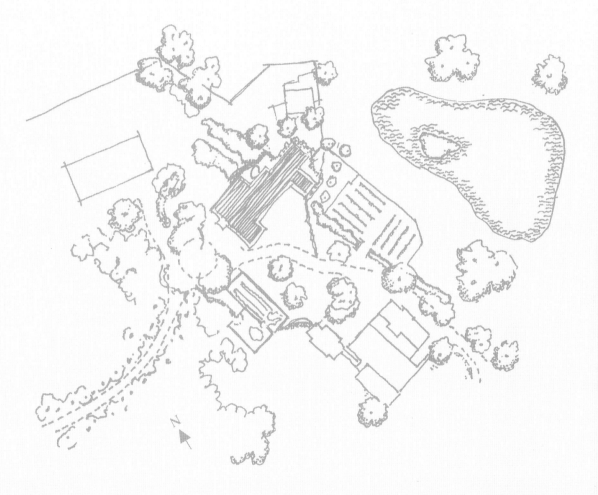

Using the topography of the rear paddock and
advice from professionals, a lake was sited to
the east of the house, where cattle once grazed.

space to be functional and prevents any one structure from becoming too dominant. It is also a windbreak for much of the southern side garden, including the rose garden.

The rose garden is a romantic mix of mainly hybrid teas and floribundas. Neatly clipped buxus and an elaeagnus hedge provide contrast and year-round green support. The rose, as many horticulturalists know, is a great leveller. Adored by many, it is one of a small group of plants, including orchids and citrus, around which groups and societies have been established. Dedication and knowledge are the two most important elements in establishing a rose garden, for once relegating the often too evident side of modern landscaping – money – to a distant third.

Dame Elisabeth's rose garden is of a good size, but is truly a gardener's garden. Dahlias and roses are grown for their blooms. Long stems are required for floral arrangements and are grown accordingly with a no-fuss attitude.

True to the era of its design and Dame Elisabeth's tastes, the garden is full of hybrid tea roses, mainly grown for fragrance, shape and the ability to be used as a specimen cut flower. My grandmother also loved this type of rose and although Beryl Baldwin's rose garden was no match for Dame Elisabeth Murdoch's, it still feels like something from my childhood.

Being a Murdoch does have advantages – in 1987, during a flight in son Rupert's helicopter, Dame Elisabeth noted that the garden was well developed to all sides but the east. A plan was devised to introduce a body of water, an element Dame Elisabeth felt had been needed for a long time. Using the topography of the rear paddock and advice from professionals, a lake was sited to the east of the house, where cattle once grazed.

Like clockwork, once the lake was dug, downpours had it filled within days. Ducks and waterfowl made their home there and many trees were planted to complete the setting. The lake has since been enlarged, becoming one of the more spectacular features of the property. In the centre stand the sculptural remnants of a eucalyptus that died after the lake's construction. Willows (*Salix babylonica*) and pin oaks (*Quercus palustris*) flank the shores, framing views and providing visitors with an interesting walk that withholds many of the landscape features from continuous view.

For extra screening a hedge of leyland cypress has been planted, as well as many more eucalypts. One interesting project is the creation of a boundary walk of *Eucalyptus maculata*. As described by the head gardener, Michael Morrison, the plan is for the walk to be used by visitors to explore the greater property. This is high priority for Cruden Farm, as it is often the focus of charity open days.

Michael is one of the most dedicated gardeners I have met, and he and Dame Elisabeth have created something special. The importance of the gardener–owner relationship is evident here – Cruden Farm may never have

Developments have taken hold in the district, and the once rural retreat has been inundated with estates containing box-like houses, a phenomenon that could not have been predicted in the Twenties.

It's hard to imagine, but in 2007 and at the tender age of 99, Dame Elisabeth was still expanding the garden, but now with the intention of finding a terminal point for it. Developments have taken hold in the district, and the once rural retreat has been inundated with dense estates containing box-like houses, a phenomenon that could not have been predicted in the 1920s, when the area was three hours slow driving south-east of Melbourne.

Either way, the garden with no boundaries now needs to develop a screen from its neighbours. Fortunately, its development as an expanding landscape has taken care of most of this. New plantings of *Quercus canariensis* and *Quercus palustris*, which surround the trees beyond the lakes, overlap to create a soft screen. This is a far better option than a conventional hedge, and the preferred method of screening if space is not a concern.

happened without that relationship, plus an understanding of climate, architecture and the fact that a garden is never a static feature.

Historically, Cruden Farm's importance stems from it being in the hands of one of Australia's great dynasties. The age of the property and the ongoing development of the garden are rare and important features. But most of all, the garden and house are a demonstration of the achievement of a symbiotic relationship between architecture and landscape. The evolution of all structures on the property has been matched by the construction of garden features and positioning of plantings. The transformation of the house from country cottage to country manor has been matched by the upscaling of trees and simplifying of landscape features, a demonstration to all that a garden is a constantly evolving phenomenon.

PREVIOUS PAGES: willows overhang the main lake, constructed in the 1980s to the east of the house – a sheep on the island keeps the grass in check. This page: Edna Walling's walled garden is always colour coded, with the mix of tones constantly changing.

COMFORT HILL
Southern Highlands, New South Wales

AN ORNAMENTAL GARDEN would have been the last thing on the minds of early colonial settlers. Subsistence farming was usually the closest one would get to horticulture, so when it comes time to establish a garden around a colonial house, it needs to be inventive yet with an understanding of what features were important in an early struggling landscape.

During colonisation, trees are the earliest features of a landscape to be established. Planted in an early garden, they provide food, shelter, windbreaks and construction materials. This is evident in many colonial properties around the world, where the older plantings are often fruit trees and/or hardy species with select timbers.

After these pioneering trees were planted and, depending on the success of the outpost, a garden may have then developed, which would have been a different space to what we know today. The first settlers would not have the knowledge of local plants, soil or environmental conditions. Hence, the garden would be a mixed bag of successful and not-so-successful plants being trialled.

The great British colonial gardens of the West Indies, for example, contain a wonderfully eclectic mix of plant material, vastly different from that grown in Europe. Many gardens were developed around the remnants of plantations, which may have grown timber crops and such exotics as date palms and rubber trees. Those palms and other tropical trees cast welcome shade across lush lawns and gardens.

In contrast, rural Australia is one of the harshest environments ever colonised. It's hot, the old soil often isn't that good and the seasons are back to front. When the stone cottage of Comfort Hill was erected in 1841 by William Morrice, I'm sure he wasn't thinking of establishing a garden. The property stands on the Hume Highway, on the way to the rural hub of Goulburn and not far from Berrima which, in colonial days, was a day and a half's ride from Sydney.

On the edge of the Southern Highlands, which has cooler winters and lower mean temperatures than Sydney, the property is surrounded by open grassland. The original house is a pretty colonial one, constructed from locally quarried stone with outbuildings of slab timber. At the front is a small veranda, and dormer windows peep through the shingle roof. The cottage and huts still stand today as important parts of the now-renovated house, but also as testament to how little those early settlers understood about their environment. The original part of the house faces east, with small courtyard rooms to the south, not the most desirable orientation in this part of the world. As well, it lacks broad eaves, deep verandas and the open ceiling space associated with warm temperate design. The world famous Queenslander style, established during the 1850s and still used today is a plantation style house that took these design features to their aesthetic and practical height.

Extensions were made in 1940 when the property changed hands, passing from the Morrices to Marjorie Davies. Her vision was to turn the once quaint cottage into a substantial house, incorporating the separate kitchen, and creating internal staff quarters.

The house didn't change hands again until 1987, when garden enthusiast Michael Ball bought it. His first changes were to restore the existing buildings and add two more rooms plus a garage. Using stone from the property for the new construction, he managed to maintain the overall aesthetic. With the house in order, Michael and his wife, Diana, went about creating a 5-hectare (12-acre) garden.

The first stage in establishing a garden in the middle of a paddock is the installation of windbreaks and trees to create boundaries. These are commonly planted on the perimeter of paddocks, but that's not always a good way to go about solving the problem. Solid buffers and lines of trees can themselves generate turbulent winds inside the area they are meant to protect. If room allows, it is often better to dissipate the wind over a wider distance through a thicker mass of varying species, with smaller trees and shrubs facing into the wind, and taller species on the leeward side.

After the house had been extended by the property's second owner in 1940, the outdoor living space was enhanced as more

The service drive to Comfort Hill, lined with lichen-covered timber slab post-and-rail fencing and a collection of eucalypts, is one that evokes a simple and very real sense of rural Australia.

of the surrounding open landscape was shut out. Michael, knowing all too well the benefits of substantial windbreaks, constructed a long stone wall to extend north of the house, protecting the garden from hot westerly winds. Inside this space the garden is further cooled by drifts of deciduous trees. At this point it is worth noting that Michael is a keen art collector, and commissioned statues of his children, immortalised playing and reading, are placed throughout this part of the garden. The stone wall inadvertently provided a

From here, the entry splits into two main drives, one a formal avenue of *Quercus palustris* running to the front of the garden and the other a curved drive that skims the edge of a lake on the way to the working part of the property.

Before I'd ever been to the garden at Comfort Hill, I had admired the formal drive from the motorway, which zooms past the property. There is not a lot to see at 110 kilometres an hour, but it is possible to make out the avenue of oaks and a freestanding

view of household windows. At Comfort Hill, on the other hand, the overwhelming emotion, to me, was one of childhood nostalgia, evoking family trips to the country.

The trees are an essential part of the overall scheme, and Michael strictly followed the design maxim of always planting in groups of three or five of the same species. One of the feature plants used is zelkova, which gives the garden a spectacular orange hue in autumn. Significant araucarias flank the house, as do quercus and silver birch.

Michael became so enthusiastic about tree growing that he started his own nursery. In a disused horse arena on the western side of the house, the nursery provides an income as well as plant material for the garden. Appreciative of the slightly unusual, it is one of the better nurseries to pick up oddities such as the very white *Betula jacquemontii* (white Himalayan birch), or giant clipped balls of teucrium.

The lake at Comfort Hill provides the garden with a much needed focal point. Very deep and carved to form two bodies of water, it also works as a water storage catchment for the garden and, bordered by a thick collection of Louisiana iris, gives colour to the garden. Grove plantings of three and five trees then frame views to the lake, many focused towards a stone rotunda situated on an island in the centre of the design. From the far side of the lake, which is skimmed by the second drive, it is possible to have a view of the rotunda supported by a thick backdrop of zelkova and elms. The view is made narrow and direct by a dense shrubbery, which offers a terminal point before the garden enters another paddock.

Aviaries are also dotted along the fringe of the lake, containing parrots, finches and quail. It's quite a serious set-up with the

A garden should provide the visitor with a sense of wellbeing, mystery or, even, a sense of being a bit naughty, as if they shouldn't be there.

humidity-free setting for espaliered apples on the western side and a backdrop for mixed shrubs sensitive to fungal issues.

Remote gardens, more than many others, take time to develop. The trees that form the basis of the garden may need to be 10 or 15 years old before a successful landscape can be constructed around them. While the trees are growing, there is plenty of time to develop a thematic plan. Comfort Hill is a mixed array of different styles, although at the appropriate places, the garden is uniquely Australian.

For me, the entry at Comfort Hill is one of the most beautiful and distinctly Australian property entries I have seen. It is basically a timber slab post-and-rail fence bordering a drive, and a collection of shortish eucalypts which look as if they are part of the scribbly gum group. It's not a grand entry like that at Cruden Farm but, instead, one that evokes a simple sense of rural Australiana, the setting much more resembling the back of Bourke than the back of Bowral.

dry stone wall bordering the drive and neighbouring paddock, letting you know that something special is behind those gates.

Entering the garden via the formal entry, you're faced with options of different drives and vistas. The house, nestled in the garden, is glimpsed through trees and shrubs. In the foreground, a rose collection in a parterre garden is aligned with an avenue of trees leading away from the central axis of the house. Although nowhere near as formal as David Hicks' garden at The Grove, it does feel rather like it, with its use of good proportions and appropriate distance.

Many people don't realise that a successful garden is one that evokes emotion. It should have some sort of ambience which provides the visitor with a sense of wellbeing, mystery or, even, a sense of being a bit naughty, as if they shouldn't be there. That's how I felt at The Grove; although I had been invited and hadn't sneaked under the fence, it felt slightly unsettling to walk on the grass or stay within

CLOCKWISE, FROM TOP LEFT: trees in a walled area were planted to provide shelter; the formal driveway, lined with an avenue of pin oaks; a shingle-roofed old hut at the rear of the house; an espaliered apple on the side of the house.

LEFT TO RIGHT: the split timber fence and stone wall are both new, but look as if they are an original part of the property, while trees to the left have been planted as a windbreak; to the south of the house, a new stone wall has been constructed.

Clockwise, from top left: detail of the split timber fence; a dry stone wall; a bench shaded by a climbing rose; the gravel driveway, wide enough for a car, links the end of the formal drive to the working areas of the house; the tools of a working garden; a white swan; an old slab hut.

aviaries containing landscape gardens of their own. Having animals in the garden is a wonderful feature and one that was endorsed by many Victorian landscapers. The Royal Botanic Gardens Sydney was, for a short time, also Sydney Zoo and, since the 1870s, New York's Central Park has been home to one of the world's most popular garden zoos.

I have always had a small passion for such things as, when I was a boy, my maternal grandfather had an octagonal aviary in his yard, and my job used to be filling the water and seed containers whenever we visited him.

Michael took the challenge of mixing his gardening and ornithological passions to new levels with the creation of a bird sanctuary. Enclosed behind a conifer hedge, it is one of the most enjoyable garden features I have seen. Created around two lakes linked by a flowing stream, the sanctuary is dedicated to water-based species such as ducks, fowl and, the pride of the collection, two white swans. Inside the enclosure is also a small mob of wallabies, and although protected from foxes and cats by a high electrified fence, this part of the landscape has a secret garden feel to it, because of the conifer hedge entry.

Colonial gardens were experiments; they had no precedents, except for their owners' imported tradition. When you enter these properties, it's nice to feel they retain something of their original setting, evoking the feel of the district. If you're planning a colonial garden, it is vital to try to utilise the existing architecture, but it is also important not to be fooled by the orientation of the house, or the arrangement of the landscape. The chances are they will be flawed, and some fresh ideas, based on an improved knowledge of environment and local conditions, will be required.

AVENUE PLANTING

While trees in general protect the house and garden in the Australian countryside, an avenue of trees from the front gate up to the house doesn't serve that practical purpose. Instead, the avenue can, at times, be purely ego driven – it's there to make a statement. There are some great avenues around, and part of the enjoyment of a long country drive comes from spotting them as they provide punctuation points in the landscape and landmarks for locals. There's a slight sense of mystery about them – without seeing what's at the end, you wonder whether you'd be disappointed. Often the grandest avenue leads to the most modest of houses.

AGRICULTURAL LIFE

A lot of country properties are still agriculturally based and that should be kept in mind when planning a garden. You don't want to feel as if you're in an oversized city garden – instead, as you wander around the garden, you want to be able to catch glimpses of paddocks and horses and other aspects of farm life. On the way in to Cruden Farm, you drive past cows and through the true agricultural side of the property, which is exactly the way it should be.

OUTBUILDINGS

On a country property, the outbuildings can often be far more interesting than the house itself. To the outsider, especially, they're a reminder that this is a farm, which can be quite an exciting prospect. Outbuildings, often rustically simple, handmade structures, should be celebrated and incorporated into the overall scheme. The garden design should never try to hide the fact, for instance, that a particular building was once an abattoir – it's part of the history of the property, and part of the whole cyclical nature of life, and the garden.

in detail

HOMESTEAD GARDENS

PROTECTIVE TREES

Quite simply, a homestead garden wouldn't exist without trees, so they are the first things that should be planted. In Australia, it's a struggle to keep anything alive, so you should choose the hardiest, toughest trees possible and let them grow up before you think of planting anything underneath. A good friend of mine built up a garden just out of peppercorn trees, which are so much part of Australian country towns – the result was very evocative. Once the trees have grown, you can start planning the garden underneath – the trees will then shelter those plants from the wind and sun, and help protect the house from the elements as well.

AUTUMN

There's something particularly lovely about autumn leaves, and about letting a tree do what it does naturally. One of the curses of the modern world is the leaf blower, a particularly annoying piece of equipment that is probably found more commonly in the city than the country – rural people have far too much to do to worry about blowing leaves from one spot to another. Getting rid of autumn leaves seems to be a rejection of the seasons; nature isn't pristine, so there's no point in pretending it is. Anyway, leaves have their place: apart from making a satisfying scrunch as you walk through them, they break down and provide nutrients to the soil.

BOUNDARIES

It's not something that city dwellers usually have to worry about, but those trying to develop a garden on a large country property have the dilemma of deciding where the garden should actually end. Too much space can be more difficult to deal with than too little. As a horticulturalist, I'd say it's all about taking a walk, doing things on a circuit, often starting and finishing with the house. There may be more than one walk – two or three may seem appropriate. The planning is never intentional, but somehow always magically seems to be quite obvious once you start looking.

ART DECO AND
MODERNIST GARDENS

With their clean lines and minimal decoration, Art Deco and modernist architecture are
not necessarily a natural fit with garden design although, treated sensitively, it can be done.

SOME STYLES OF architecture don't naturally lend themselves to gardens, and Art Deco and modernism would be two of the most obvious in that respect. Simply put, these two styles of architecture valued functionalism and the latest technology, and rejected decoration and ornament – on the surface, at least, the simpler the better. Glass, steel and concrete were the materials of choice, and none of those would seem to be a good match with the vagaries of plant and tree growth. With clean lines being the overriding architectural feature, it's hard to imagine a garden scheme that fits into that way of thinking. Do you go with it, or fight against it? That's what garden designers of the time wrestled with or, in many cases, decided not to even think about, preferring to avoid having anything to do with the land around Art Deco or modernist houses. Part of the problem was that those styles rejected the past to come up with a thoroughly new, or 'modern', design. Was it possible for garden designers to do the same – could they throw out everything they'd done before and start again? Would sweeping lawns make way for great expanses of concrete, and what would happen to the garden bed?

Over the years, many approaches have been taken with such architecture, and it's something that still comes up when dealing with today's contemporary designs, so many of which are based on modernist principles.

As far as I'm concerned, there are three basic ways in which a garden can be designed to suit an Art Deco or modernist house.

The first is to contrast the simplicity of the house with exotica. The simple, flat walls of the architecture can be used as a blank canvas to showcase the unusual. *Dracaena draco* (dragon's blood tree), palms, pandanus and succulents, along with strikingly coloured plants such as hibiscus and cordylines, are all species that, when planted en masse, add a feel of exotica, which only the harsh lines of modernism can support. A combination of differing plants, such as perhaps bamboo and hibiscus in a bed of clivia, pittosporum and ginger, is the best way to achieve an exotic aesthetic. For most landscapes, this grouping may be a little overpowering, but sited within a simple concrete landscape it works well.

The second approach is to match the simplicity of the architecture with minimalism. On many such landscapes, the job is already half done, as it was common for architects to request their creations be left uncomplicated by the addition of fussy surrounds. In other cases, owners haven't known how to landscape around their 'modern' homes, and it's been easier to do nothing.

Typically designed with a long, low profile, Deco or modernist houses are well suited to low, lateral landscape design. Extensive flat lawns and ground covers, along with low terraced retaining walls or berms (if needed), suit most designs, as do large expanses of stone or concrete for entertaining areas. Somehow, those broad areas of solid material give the often domineering architecture a sense of scale and perspective. The planting needs to be equally strong.

Strong planting can be achieved by making a statement with a single specimen or by massing together a monoculture plant selection. Sticking with the low, broad theory, a specimen oak, box or jacaranda will be of the right scale to provide impact. Mass plantings can also work – squares of clipped escallonia or buxus, approximately equal to the length and height of the house, can look dramatic. Another approach would be to plant large drifts of ivy to form a shadow line for the structure.

The third approach is the re-created natural landscape or anti-garden. Although he was not a modernist, several of American architect Frank Lloyd Wright's houses are situated in landscapes that have been reworked to appear to be natural, with the building looking as if it has been dropped from the heavens without disturbing a single plant or tree. His most famous house, Falling Water, not only appears to leave the surroundings undisturbed but also lets the flow of Bear Creek follow its natural path. This is an exciting place to visit but apparently not the most comfortable house to live in, as some of those natural elements have wreaked havoc on the building itself. The idea behind the anti-garden is to contrast nature and the lines of the architecture, a design theory used in many modern settings. While it may look untamed, the anti-garden, of the three approaches, is often the most difficult to achieve. Creating nature doesn't come without enormous effort – it's often a case of building mountains and other landforms before you think about planting. When done convincingly, though, the effect can be spectacular, and provide the perfect setting for minimalist architecture.

Black and white chequerboard paving at Wyldefel Gardens includes a floating marble step. This was the client's idea and, with the shadow line formed, gives a contemporary twist to the design.

WYLDEFEL GARDENS
Potts Point, Sydney

NOT ALL SUCCESSFUL period gardens need to exist upon acres and acres of land. A courtyard, terrace or even a rooftop may adopt period styling. It is, however, a sad fact that the more modern a property is, the more likely it is to be small. The simple rules of development state that for a person to make money from property, it needs to be chopped up and developed. A large estate can be divided several times until it ends up as a very 'ungardenable' concrete landscape of modern apartment living or 'a hole in the wall', as my father would put it.

Almost all the world's great cities have embraced the apartment; high density living is our future. The downside of this is that gardens are disappearing. An apartment can't have a garden...or can it?

With no historic precedent, the styling of apartments in Sydney is as open-ended as you would find in New York or even in the cities of a developing super-nation like China. The goal of many apartments in Sydney is to have a view of the harbour, the beach or the city itself. This phenomenon has led to the development of many apartment blocks in the city's eastern suburbs, particularly on the three peninsulas stretching into the harbour.

As Potts Point has the highest population density in the country, the local government has dubbed it the 'New York' of Australia. It's a bustling community and was one of the first places in Sydney to succumb to high-rise development. Probably the first apartment block in the district was Kingsclere, built in 1912 and, although I like it as an ornate Edwardian structure, its mammoth square design of brick and stone set the standard for the size and scope of works that would be followed by almost all other developers.

One group of apartments, Wyldefel Gardens, situated at the northern end of Potts Point, stands out from the crowd, and it was here that I was fortunate enough to design and build a garden. The complex, built on the site of an old harbourside mansion, is unusual because it is virtually invisible from the street, becoming part of the landscape, rather than dominating it. It was the vision of William Crowle, a patron of the arts, who observed contemporary housing outside the town of Oberammergau in Germany, appreciating the way it utilised the landscape to construct livable, beautiful high-density housing.

Officially designed by architect John Brogan, the layout is quite simple. Apartments are built on terraces stretching down the slope of a hill; each apartment supports another, with the roof of the forward apartment supplying the garden for the one behind. Additional apartments are squeezed below some of the rooftop ones and, although joked about as dungeons, they have a lovely outlook to a communal garden courtyard in the centre of the complex. Two 'wings' of apartments terrace down the hill and create the central court which, when constructed in 1936, cascaded down to the water. The property was considered almost a resort, with a tennis court, swimming pool and boathouse.

The architectural styling that had inspired Crowle was Art Deco, or Maritime Art Deco to be more precise, with the design of an ocean liner inspiring such features as curvaceous stern-like walls, porthole windows and clean rendered walls. It was a common design style in many beachside and harbourside suburbs, but not in Potts Point.

The original mansion was retained during the redevelopment, and remained the

PREVIOUS PAGES: the view from the back of the exotica garden, which contains *Hedychium greenii*, kentia palms and *Pittosporum tobira* 'Miss Muffett'. These pages, clockwise from left: cymbidium orchid; a light designed by Tyrone Dearing and David Ellem; clipped buxus on the terrace; frangipani.

house of William Crowle, with the central courtyard garden of the apartments allowing direct access from the house to the harbour. The onset of the Second World War, however, forced major changes to the property. The naval base of nearby Garden Island required immediate expansion for new warehousing and dry docking, and the waterfront land of Wyldefel Gardens was compulsorily acquired, leaving the property surrounded by naval buildings and shipyards. The tennis court and pool were demolished, and the boathouse was deconstructed and moved to a new location on the other side of the harbour.

I first came across the property through an invitation from interior designer David Ellem, whose client had been thinking of buying one of the rare rooftop garden apartments. We were just going in for a quick look before the sale.

First impressions are important with almost every house, but not with Wyldefel Gardens. The once amazing mansion that looked over the property had long been removed and replaced with an uninspiring block of flats, leaving the entry to Wyldefel via the parking bays and garaging. Only a smallish corridor adjacent to the neigbouring building allows access to the central court.

Once inside the property, the atmosphere changes, and you can forget the car park and towering apartments, and you can even forget that you're in the most densely populated area of Australia. Between the two-tiered runs of apartments are the bones of the original garden as set out in 1936. Trees such as a black bean, *Camellia japonica* and fruiting avocado have reached their full potential, providing shade and an ambient cooling environment. Understorey plantings are typical of the

exotic trend of the period and comprise philodendron, aspidistra, justicia and clivia. Palms such as kentias also feature, as does the palm-like giant strelitzia, *Strelitzia nicolai*.

Time has sadly taken its toll on a number of the structural elements. Many of the original bluestone steps have been replaced with concrete or supposedly similar products. Tree roots have lifted and cracked many of the paths, and in other locations the installation of services has meant parts of the garden have been destroyed. Overall, though, the layout is similar to early photos of the property and, if someone wanted to, it would be a small task to restore the garden. The apartment gardens in the complex, however, had not fared so well.

There are six apartments – three on either tier – which have the large rooftop terraces. The one I worked on was in the centre level on the northern tier. As we had discovered,

the apartment was spacious and, with a few judicious changes, well designed, but the garden was a surprise. What greeted you as you walked through the maritime doors were unevenly laid concrete pavers stuck to the roof membrane. Beyond that was a concrete and brick edge supporting a large square lawn of kikuyu, couch and buffalo grass, across the rear of which ran a bed containing a frangipani, mixed shrubs and a 4-metre (13-foot) cumquat. How a cumquat managed to get 4 metres tall in 300mm (one foot) of soil I wasn't quite sure, but I knew it wouldn't be good for the downstairs neighbour.

The agent who sold the property had instructed the previous owner to tart things up a little before the sale, and along with the plain garden came a large plastic water feature, white gravel mulch, concrete pots of bamboo and a rather annoying set of ugly bromeliads.

David Ellem attacked the interior with an all-or-nothing attitude. He had worked for the owner on his previous residence and proved that nothing can beat outright style. Flooring and joinery were created from American light oak and the bathrooms from calacutta marble. The furniture was selected to suit the Art Deco space and fit well into the large rooms.

A similar attitude was required for the garden. Existing landscape features needed to be removed; all existing paving was taken up, and the grass, soil and all plants had gone well beyond even recycling. However, a problem arose when the roof was finally clean – the

existing membrane, created from tar and copper strips, had either worn away or become damaged during the excavation. This would not be so much of a problem in most gardens but, in this case, the garden was the roof of the apartment below. Two weeks of cleaning and applying waterproofing measures played havoc with the work schedule but did mean the new garden is assured of a long life.

Its design is fairly simple. Paving extends across the rear of the apartment to a step, where a lawn continues to the edge of the yard. Running the length of the lawn on the northern side, a garden has been installed to

Once inside the property, the atmosphere changes, and you can forget the car park and towering apartments, and you can even forget that you're in the most densely populated area of Australia.

Simplicity, in the form of the minimum of elements and a monochromatic scheme, is the approach taken for the rooftop garden at Wyldefel Gardens. The roof of this apartment is the rooftop garden of the apartment above.

screen the neighbouring apartments and, in a carefully selected spot on the lawn, a solitary frangipani has been planted.

During my time working for *The Sydney Morning Herald*, I wrote a piece on how to approach Art Deco garden design. One item I mentioned was how such houses suit minimalism and a strong lateral presence. The client at Wyldefel held me to this statement, which made items like the presentation of the lawn and solitary frangipani so important.

The paving selected for the garden is black nero marble and white carrara marble

nature of the overall design and adds a subtle quirk to what would have been a plain step.

The shadow line, which also serves the practical purpose of concealing the drains from the paving, was constructed by forming a concrete ledge 100mm (four inches) deep and covering it in the marble. Exposed drains and services are a pet hate of mine, and I was glad when we came up with a solution. In most of my gardens, I go out of my way to hide the mechanics of the build – to my mind, a garden should be an illusion, a vision of paradise, often created where something should not

some pink brugmansia. 'Wilder's White' and 'Apple Blossom' are two of my favourite hibiscus cultivars; they're both tough and fast-growing but, more importantly, were around during the Thirties and look particularly well suited to the architecture.

The completed garden looks simple and well designed, but there is nothing easy about constructing a garden three floors above the ground. Landscapers, trudging up and down stairs with 20kg (44lb) bags of cement on their shoulders, built this garden. An 18-tonne crane, stretched to full reach, delivered the plants and the 36 tonnes of soil, which had to be removed and then replaced. New technology has a place here – lightweight expanded concrete walls were constructed to save precious kilos, and the garden was wired for lights, and irrigated using concealed drip lines.

This garden at Wyldefel serves two purposes. The first is to screen the towering apartments to the north, while the second is to provide the owner with a beautiful arrangement of plants.

laid in a square chequerboard pattern. Such a design has been used in many different periods, but not often outside, or in 700 x 700mm (27 x 27 inch) slabs. With the interior designer, I visited several historic properties using similar stone to make sure the aesthetic would turn out the way I had hoped. The result speaks for itself; it is an amazing finish, but does require regular maintenance to retain a strong colour and toughness.

Forming the front edge of the lawn and completing the paving is a carrara step with feature shadow line. I would love to take credit for adding the overhang on the step to create the shadow line, but it was the client's brilliant idea. Inspired by the lawn in the centre of Sydney's historic Mint building, now also the head office of the Historic Houses Trust, the client came up with the idea of adding what is really a very clever and modern element to the garden. The shadow line reinforces the lateral

exist. This is the ultimate illustration of that, as gardens should not appear on rooftops.

This garden serves two purposes. The first is to screen the towering apartments to the north, the second to provide the owner with a beautiful arrangement of plants. Both minimalism and exoticism complement Art Deco architecture, the clean lines of which are matched by low horizontal stark forms, such as that of the paving, lawn and frangipani. On the other hand, it can also be contrasted by huge leaves and varying forms.

For height in the garden I planted *Bambusa multiplex*, kentia palms and a *Michelia doltsopa*. All three plants have vastly different foliage. To provide some continuity to the garden, a continual understorey planting of *Pittosporum tobira* 'Miss Muffett' and Belgian hybrid clivia was installed. The garden, however, lacked density. To fix this, I tracked down two old hibiscus cultivars and planted

The final touches were added by the interior designer. In keeping with the exotic theme, Chinese urns with cymbidium orchids were used to frame the rear doors; clipped Japanese box balls provide some structure and a potted hibiscus 'Apple Blossom' helps fill out the paved area. The furniture was kept light and simple, the idea being that, although it is beautiful, it should be fairly invisible, so as not to detract from the overall landscape.

The rooftop gardens at Wyldefel were never great – in the early photos, all you see are concrete pavers and grass. They were a great idea, though, and over the years residents have attempted some interesting gardens, while others have fallen a little short. The construction of this garden was about, first, finding the best elements that gardening of the time had to offer, and then drawing inspiration from those elements and interpreting them to create a brilliant, modern outdoor space.

PREVIOUS PAGES: the terrace at Wyldefel Gardens, with its backdrop of golden robinia, which forms part of the communal area of the apartment complex. Opposite: *Hedychium greenii* in the exotica garden.

CHEQUERBOARD PAVING

There are pluses and minuses to using marble outside; for a start, the chequerboard pattern looks stunning, if you can maintain the stone. However, by trial and error, I've discovered black marble fades in the sun, and there's not a lot you can do about it. It does get to a point, however, where it stops fading, but will never be the intense colour it once was. The lesson when choosing stone is to be very careful of its properties and the way it reacts to ultraviolet light. It's been underground for millions of years and some of it isn't too happy to have the sun on it – the problem seems to be greater with the darker coloured stones.

MONOTONE

Art Deco architecture and monotone go hand in hand, and a lot of people find the concept a curse. Monotone isn't just monotonous, they believe, but the sky blue façade of an Art Deco house, for instance, is impossible to work with. The way I look at it is the monotone – say, sky blue – pushes you into more exciting options. The enemy of blue is orange, so instead of fighting against it, go with it – think of that façade as a big blank canvas and plant lots of bold, orange-red plants against it. You really have to think about what to plant: you might find it limiting to start with but it can be liberating to focus your attention and force yourself to look at plants you wouldn't have otherwise considered.

LAWNS

Art Deco was the era of lawns, which may have something to do with the fact that it was around the time the motor mower came into production, and the peace of weekend mornings was broken by the drone of that suburban machine. The lawn phenomenon went too far, becoming the ultimate minimalist statement – a lawn with a concrete path down it is not good design, it's purely sterile. Think of a lawn as a blank canvas needing a frame. It's no good extending the lawn up to the house – a horizontal extreme against a vertical extreme looks too stark. An easy rule is that a lawn shouldn't butt up against anything higher than a bench – a low retaining wall in front of the house could provide the required frame.

in detail

ART DECO AND MODERNIST GARDENS

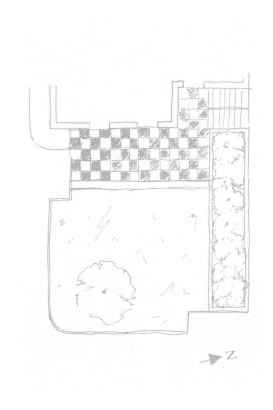

MINIMALISM

There's no room for error in a minimalist garden – it's a fine line between creating a successful one and looking as if you haven't tried. To avoid the latter, structure needs to be present, and it's quite a mathematical feat to work that out. Replicate the geometry of the buildings in the garden, wherever possible. It's often about finding the midpoint between the various features on the buildings – doors and windows and so on – and projecting them outwards. Dimensions have to be carefully calculated: garden beds need to be just the right size, and lawns and different levels perfectly set out. And when you're cutting the lawn, mow in the same direction to create precise stripes. It's all in the detail.

EXOTICISM

One way of dealing with an Art Deco house is to provide extreme contrast to the minimal nature of the building and go for clashing tones and textures. Complement exotic plant material with buxus, suitably shaped. There are a few catchy cultural plants particularly associated with Art Deco architecture – hibiscus is one. The colours of the hibiscus flower look stunning next to the house. Another is *Dracaena drago* (dragon's blood tree), and then there's strelitzia, or bird of paradise, which instantly looks exotic. Kentia palms are another option and so, too, is bamboo, which is quite minimalist and linear in itself.

FRANGIPANI

Frangipani is one tree that can be grown from giant cuttings. You can stick a 5-metre-tall (15-foot-tall) cutting into the ground and, as long as it's stable and the soil is free draining, there's no problem. It's an incredibly hardy tree – I've twisted and broken off lower stems and roots to force the plant into growing in 300mm (1 foot) of soil, as was the case at Wyldefel Gardens. Roots naturally grow laterally – there's no point in a tree growing deep roots unless there's a good water source down there. All nutrients and moisture are close to the surface, and so that's where the roots stay. Only the carrot has an old fashioned tap root.

DETAILS

In a period garden, attention to detail in all features, from paths
and driveways to tennis courts and swimming pools, is absolutely essential.

LAWNS

ALTHOUGH ONE OF the simpler garden elements, the lawn is a difficult feature to design. The size, type, shape and contour of a lawn can alter the way a garden is perceived. A large expanse in front of a house may give prominence to the architecture, while a small lawn needs to have a focal point.

A lawn is an odd part of horticulture, as it is both ornamental and utilitarian. In most cases, a lawn comes about as a result of the need for an entertaining space, a space for the children or access to other parts of the garden.

The size of the lawn needs to reflect the size of the house or the feature it supports. A large lawn needs to be associated with a large house, or with plantings that need to be viewed from a distance to realise the full picture. Grand lawns such as those adjacent to the houses at Stourhead (page 58), Hatfield House and Ditchley Park all suit their surroundings.

Visitors to Bronte House (page 104) have often commented on the lawn at the centre of the carriageway. In the centre of the lawn stands a Norfolk Island pine which, in spite of its large trunk, does not diminish the view to the house. The surrounding gardens and drive frame the lawn, only ending at the house's façade. In a dense suburban location, the freedom to have an expansive view is rare, and this helps with the 'wow' factor as guests enter the property.

The main key to the size of a lawn is restraint, which also needs to be used when it comes to lawn features. That extra planting of buxus around a tree, or bulbs rising up in the foreground can alter the meaning of the lawn. A lawn full of features often becomes overpowering and loses its primary purpose as a supporting element of a greater landscape. This is, however, different for a meadow, which is designed to be an explosion of texture, colour and interaction. A meadow should be felt, smelt and moved through, and never overlooked.

TENNIS COURTS

TENNIS COURTS ARE often relegated to the back of a property, as they are utilitarian spaces serving no aesthetic purpose. The best part of the court is the fence – a fantastic space for creating a vertical garden. Climbing plants, such as rose, clematis and stephanotis, look stunning against it, negating any misgivings you may have about the big green hole at the bottom of the garden. That expanse of nothing does allow light into the garden, but apart from that, it's difficult to say anything positive about a tennis court.

Most successful courts I've seen have been hidden – Rofford Manor's (page 146) is slightly sunken, lowering the height of the fence. A hedge of the same height around the perimeter serves to make it less imposing. At Ingleneuk (page 136), the court, with its chicken wire and timber fence, is more decorative than most.

Unless you're a serious player, the court will probably be used infrequently. Hiring a court may be more practical, but for those determined to have their own, it's important to think about the surface. I don't approve of supergrass in a period garden, as it looks far too modern. Grass is the best option but, for ease of maintenance, clay or stabilised lime are other possibilities.

Early tennis courts were concrete with oxidised concrete lines – they look the part in a heritage garden, but are not great on the knees. Asphalt is softer but doesn't look good, while stabilised lime is, apart from grass, the best option: it looks fine and is easy on the joints.

PREVIOUS PAGES: the sloping top terrace at Rona, showing Queensland blue couch lawn, camphor laurel trees, camellias and gordonia.
This page: Cruden Farm, looking across a drift of plectranthus towards the sunken tennis court and a paddock.

PREVIOUS PAGES: the tennis court at Rona, with backdrop of a cupressus hedge and vibrantly coloured tibouchina. This page, left to right: at the entry to Ingleneuk, unobtrusive brick was selected for the paving; the pea gravel forecourt at the old front of La Foce.

PAVING

AS PAVING HAS to withstand being walked on or driven over, selecting the right material requires much greater thought than many other garden elements – it is not purely a matter of aesthetics. Durability, colour, size and texture are all important factors to consider.

The shape of the paved surface is one decision that can't be avoided. For inspiration, I look at the style of the house and at how the area is used, for it is one thing to design something that looks great but another to have it work. Simplicity is often the best remedy. On my travels through Europe, I found that many of the more significant houses fill a space with gravel or hoggin, and draw the boundaries from the width of the building, or frame it by significant planting. The formal entry to Haseley Court (page 76) is an excellent example of how a simple material, geometrically laid in front of symmetrical architecture, can work. The lines of the Georgian façade are projected into the landscape by the paving, reinforcing the dominance of the house over the landscape. The use of gravel chip is clever, as it is hard-wearing and, when laid en masse, becomes an unbroken entity rather than a collection of small stones.

The concept of individual pieces of material working as one is common in larger scale landscapes. Essentially, bitumen and concrete are also a collection of tightly held particles and can be an effective material in a modern context. I'm biased towards gravel driveways, liking the sound of crunchy footsteps after it's been raked.

Along with its aesthetics and durability, gravel is also cheap but, unlike other cost efficient solutions, has become immune to 'material snobbery'. Whether it is now tradition that over larger spaces we use gravel paving or if it is a

conscious decision over other material choices, the fact remains that it is extremely popular.

When using quarried stone, the simpler the design the better the outcome. Detailed patterning draws your eye to the material, which may look out of place unless it perfectly fits the architecture. Of course, if there is existing stonework and the situation suits, replicating the original is a great idea.

Smooth cut random dimensioned local stone often works well in heritage gardens. A smooth cut stone is safe, very easy to walk on and the random nature of the pieces shows a nondescript pattern that can be used adjacent to many other architectural types. Sandstone, limestone and varying marbles can all be used in this way.

Brick paving is tricky, as it is associated with certain eras. The bricks need to be either of the same period as the architecture, or earlier, giving the illusion that the garden was constructed when the house was built or, romantically, from materials found on site. It is a challenge to find bricks in significant numbers to carry out the job and, in many recent projects, I have used modern brick paving of inoffensive colours and textures.

Brickwork detail is also important. Later architecture, especially Art Deco, may require highly detailed brickwork, such as mortared joints and patterning. Older Italian architecture will also use patterned brickwork but doesn't require such clean, sharp lines. The relaxed style also allows for more creativity to be shown, which is an enjoyable way to construct a garden.

Every product has its place and whereas, for instance, gravel is the material of choice for true heritage works, concrete may be a more obvious choice with modernist architecture. It is often a challenge, but personal tastes do need to take a back seat when it comes to period garden design.

PATHS

PATHS THROUGH A garden are much more than just a means of getting from one place to the next. They can create mystery and a sense of adventure; they may be used to channel the eye to a focal point or away from another garden or landscape element. Depending on the period of architecture and several other factors, the path will take on varying forms.

The decision about the shape and size of a paved space in a period style garden is already made for you. Architecture, topography and function will always determine whether the approach to the residence is straight or meandering, whether the forecourt or courtyard is large or small and whether the overall layout is organic or one of formality. I don't know of one heritage garden that, topography permitting, has a paved surface based upon a naturalistic setting. Curved paths and forecourts are always based upon some sort of geometry; the tangent of a curve, the radius around a tree or the dimension of the front door to the stone central pillar halved and projected 45 degrees from the nearest wall. There is always a reason.

In early French and Italianate gardens, the geometry of the landscape contained symmetrical axes extending as far as the eye could see, arranging the garden in a series of grids, which would be met by other long paths and axes. The infill spaces between the primary paths would be left to more intricate designs, acting as a contrast to the simplicity of the axes and layout.

The English Landscape movement chose to ignore the French way of gardening and, with this, the garden path became exactly that. The person who coined the phrase 'to lead someone up the garden path' must surely have been referring to an English Landscape garden.

Often moving from shade to light, from meadows and bulbs to shrubs and trees, an English garden path developed during the eighteenth century, more from desire lines than from manmade construction, and walking on it became more of an adventure than purely a journey. Ideally, the path follows the contours, banking to places of interest, but appearing to happen upon them as if by accident. Re-creating nature successfully is a very hard thing to do. The idealised Landscape garden at Stourhead (page 58) is one of the best examples, with the pathway around the main lake meandering seemingly randomly past the follies and feature plantings, more like a goat track than a crafted path.

Unlike a French path in which the axis is often spelled out by the architecture, an English Landscape path has options. Do you go around or in front of the stand of trees; do you take the direct route or snake over the landscape?

Although every site is different, there are some rules that need to be obeyed. A winding path mustn't just turn by accident. Whether it is just to follow a sloping contour or to avoid an object, a path needs a reason to change direction. In an established landscape, a new path might avoid a stand of trees or some existing architecture. But in a new blank landscape, these features need to be added. Planting a stand of trees is the easiest and cheapest way to give meaning to a winding path.

Heading across a slope is preferable to climbing one and, although it's the longer route, can develop into a feature within itself. A quintessential Tuscan scene shows a zigzag road created by the local co-operative and the Origo family of La Foce. The road was meant to be the easiest route to the top of the hill opposite the great garden, and symbolised the completion of

THIS PAGE, CLOCKWISE FROM LEFT: zigzag road at La Foce was built in the 1930s for utilitarian reasons, but has become a feature in the Tuscan countryside; a gravel pathway on the way to the great lake at Stourhead; stone paths lined with perennials at Rofford Manor.

all the hard work creating arable lands for the community and farm.

A long path needs points of reflection. It needs to mean a lot more than a way of getting from A to B. A path should have a place to sit, or to be removed from the journey. In a romantic garden, this may be a spot to sit down to enjoy a short view of a body of water or even a distant vista. In a more rigid and formal garden, a seat immersed within the formality may be a feature in itself, where one can admire the workmanship of the garden.

The landscape in its entirety should only be viewed in select locations along a path. Whether formal or informal, a landscape should always keep a sense of mystery about it. Even in a garden such as the one at the palace of Versailles, the dominant view down the central axis and onto the grand canal does not reveal the ponds and fountains within the beech hedging, nor does it reveal the many finer details that can be seen when looking back to the palace.

A more English garden, however, works with the contours rather than removing them, and will often provide a visitor with a glimpse of their destination before revealing it in its entirety. The glimpse of a feature is often just as important as the final approach, as it creates a sense of anticipation, with the thrill of the chase being part of the journey. Correctly framing the vista is vital, and involves a lot more than merely positioning a tree either side of the view. In a relaxed garden, asymmetrical design can be observed, and plantings to the middle and foreground will be far more effective. In a formal garden, the correct width of a view can be created by planting an avenue, with only the length of the avenue providing the spread of the vista.

DRIVES

THE DRIVE IS the main entrance to almost every great garden. The first impression will often be the determining factor in any long-lasting memory of the visit. A drive needs to be both a utilitarian and decorative feature, but often falls prey to becoming more of one than the other. You'll either have a pretty drive that can't be used or an efficient drive that becomes virtually a highway. Designing a drive for a city compared to a country property is a vastly different experience; where a rural drive may pass through separate stages, from a paddock entry to the forecourt of a house and needs to be treated accordingly, a city drive will often require the highest detail throughout, as it will find use even as an entertainment space.

The newly installed drive at the entrance to the great Sydney garden of Rona (page 90) is one of the most magical entries to a property I have ever come across. Designed to meander through the existing mature trees without affecting their health, the drive becomes not only a practical solution but also, inadvertently, a very pretty one.

Dame Elisabeth Murdoch's driveway at Cruden Farm (page 190) was described by noted designer and gardener David Hicks as one of the most beautiful he had seen. Like many other rural drives, it is made from crushed stone and gravel, but is surrounded by a unique avenue of gums that fill the drive with scattered, twisted light and a pinkish hue.

A drive should feel part of the garden rather than of the street. A mistake often made with larger driveways is the installation of guttering and a surface not dissimilar from the nearby street – no one wants their drive to look as if it has been built by the local council.

The compacted gravel driveway to Hodges Barn has a romantic feel to it as it dips and turns with the contours of the land, approaching the side, rather than the front, of the house.

POOLS

VERY RARELY IS a swimming pool an original feature of a heritage garden. Some waterfront properties had bath houses or converted rock pools; some more elaborate homes were even developed near springs, but those were used more as a bathing feature than for relaxation.

In Australia, pools and an aquatic upbringing are cultural institutions. Although we never had a pool when I was growing up, one was only a hurdle of a fence or bicycle ride away.

My great-grandfather had a 0.4 hectare (one acre) garden in Sydney in the 1950s; the focal point was a pool, one of the few private ones in the area at the time. Placed within spitting distance of the bay, it had no filtration equipment and was filled with sea water at high tide. No chemicals were added and, after use, the water was emptied back into the bay at low tide.

The pool was made from rendered brickwork reinforced with concrete and painted lemon yellow, which turned the water a greenish tone. Although simple to operate, the pool had its problems: algae formed on the walls, requiring cleaning whenever it was emptied, and the walls needed painting every year.

Modern pools are far more complex but are also user-friendly. Advances in design and technology have meant that a pool can take on the appearance of un-pool-like landscape elements, a trait I find useful for heritage work.

A swimming pool in a garden plays a far greater role than just a place for swimming. A pool can be a focal point, providing an ambient feeling of tranquillity or a place for action and excitement. Children are often the instigators of the swimming pool and therefore the main users of the space, meaning that it cannot be just an ornamental feature but must often contain supposed requirements of modern life – spas, benches and heated water to name a few.

Modern conveniences also come with modern inconveniences. For a pool to be used, it needs to interact with the house or be given a dedicated area. When I position a pool, I try to integrate it into the landscape as much as possible. By utilising various architectural elements, the pool appears as an existing feature. A walled garden is a gift to anyone proposing to install a pool; the existing boundaries of a remnant landscape feature not only provide the perfect frame but also create a safe environment.

Replicating existing landscape features is also a good method of fitting a pool into a landscape. The swimming pool at Ingleneuk (page 136) uses a sandstone coping that blends into the adjacent entertaining area. All garden paths and retaining walls are sandstone, so it was only fitting to repeat the material for the pool.

Safety regulations are some of the most difficult elements of pool design to work with. Integrating obtrusive fencing is especially troublesome when working with heritage design. Styles often clash and what is technically correct for a pool isn't great for a garden.

Integrating the pool fence into an existing wall and minimising the amount of fence required is the obvious solution. A change in height may also be useful, as an elevated pool with a sheer retain supporting the structure complies as a fence of the equivalent height.

Ultra-modern fencing has been the preferred option of many heritage architects, who feel that any new feature added to a heritage one should be modern minimalism, clearly defining a new item overlaid on an existing original. It works brilliantly, with striking architecture and many heritage styles going hand in hand to produce a chic aesthetic.

LEFT TO RIGHT: tiles in the pool at Boomerang spell out 'MR', initials of a previous owner; the formal, rectangular shape of the pool at La Foce matches the simplicity of the garden's overall Renaissance design.

PONDS

IN GRAND PROPERTIES, water and ponds were seen as symbols of power and wealth. In less flamboyant gardens, a pond was either completely out of the question or purely utilitarian. For this reason, I've always approached pond design on a domestic scale with the idea that it should look like a cistern or tank rather than something purely ornamental.

Like other landscape elements, the construction of a pond and the materials used can be derived from other architectural elements, such as a cut of stone or type of moulding.

Modern equipment lets you achieve many more effects than was possible in the past. Submersible pumps, for instance, allow for great flexibility and, in most cases, do away with the need for expert hydrological engineering advice.

Waterproofing with modern sealants is also much easier and, where once a pond would have relied upon the entire structure being solid, now we can create a façade of the desired material and a structure of more common materials.

Existing ponds can be renovated but, in almost all situations, will need work – although things in the past were designed to last a lifetime, they have often lasted several lifetimes by the time today's gardener and designer get to them.

The main pond at Sydney's Boomerang (page 172) is an original feature of the front garden. In keeping with the house, the pond was designed along the central axis of the house in an Alhambra style. The bottom is lined in blue square tiles and its sides in green ones. In contrast, sandstone coping reflects some of the garden's more traditional materials. Over the years, large trees surrounding the pond had cracked and lifted its floor. Roots were entering it through the rendered brick walls and the

existing plumbing, although renovated, had seen better days.

To solve the issue of maintaining the original design intent and updating the pond, its floor was raised over the existing tiles. The new floor hosts all the conduit and piping required for lights and plumbing, and solves the problem of leaking. Matching tiles were laid and, although the fountain, fitted in the early Eighties, is an abomination, it was retained as a centrepiece.

Although a pond should usually suit the property, an exception is the addition of an antique one. It can be very difficult to get right and so shouldn't be chosen on a whim. Thought should go into how the new element will interact with existing landscape features. The material, colour and even the way the water relates to the surrounding landscape are all important. Acoustically, a pond can be a tranquil haven, as the gentle sounds of water are very soothing. Great care needs to be taken so that it does not sound like a torrent or become annoyingly faint.

When it was decided that a feature was needed at the newly created entry to Ingleneuk (page 136), a pond was an obvious choice. The problem was there was no construction method or precedent for a circular pond in the property. Respected heritage architect Clive Lucas's solution was to build one with the aesthetic of carved sandstone. Although there is no such design on site, the simplicity of it ensures the pond does not clash with surrounding elements.

Looking after a pond is easier than it once was. Modern technology, including ultraviolet light cylinders, filtration equipment and submersible pumps, are useful in all applications. Like many other aspects of a garden, it's all about using the equivalent of smoke and mirrors to create an idealised, if somewhat imperfect, world.

THIS PAGE, LEFT TO RIGHT: Rofford Manor pond, surrounded by low buxus hedges, has the appearance of a cistern; the pond at Bronte House, with its cast iron fountain, is planted with iris, water lily and duckweed. Following pages: pleached linden, with a footing of buxus, at Rofford Manor.

WALLS

A GARDEN DIVIDED by walls into rooms can make for a very interesting landscape, as the walls not only have aesthetic appeal, but can also improve the horticultural features of a garden and change its immediate environment. However, the construction of a garden wall needs to be carefully considered.

Aesthetically, I will often design a wall based upon materials I find around the existing architecture. That's not to say that if the house is made of brick, the garden wall should be, but there may be a primary construction material, such as a rubble footing on the house or a shed made from stone, that can act as a catalyst.

The walls in the garden at Hodges Barn (page 124) work with the house. Made by Italian prisoners of war during the Second World War, the stone walls have a relaxed feel to them and match the stonework on the house. Hodges Barn is exactly what the name suggests – a barn – and it feels as if the walls could have been some sort of agricultural extension to that, such as yards for cattle or horses, which have since been turned into a garden.

One downside of a garden wall is that it may cast shade into a garden, or reduce the flow of air into a space, making it more humid and therefore prone to fungal disease and pests. The hidden problem of a walled garden, though, is its cost. In today's gardening world, the top paid tradesman is always the stonemason who, charging by the square yard or metre, earns more money in two hours than a lowly weed-pulling gardener would in a day.

Of course, a wall can also actually become the garden, with climbing plants, mosses and espaliered plants looking stunning on a truly structural backdrop. The solid stone or masonry structure provides contrast to the foliage, and even a hint of the wall peeking through a dense mass of Boston ivy is all it takes.

FENCES

NOT ENOUGH THOUGHT goes into fencing these days. The list of available materials is endless, and how you use them is limited only by the imagination. A garden fence, in most cases, needs to be an interesting yet invisible part of the property, and the best example of this, of course, is the English estate fence.

Made from flat bar and rod, the estate fence is possibly the most basic garden fence in the world. It is not particularly secure, and is prone to being bent and twisted by livestock trying to reach greener grass, but is a beautifully delicate yet masculine garden feature. At Rofford Manor (page 146), the fence has a few modern additions that have been used to join it to a stone ha-ha via a sweet hinged pedestrian gate. At Stourhead (page 58), a kissing-style gate, made from a straight and bent piece of fencework, has been inserted into the estate fence.

In a modern landscape, though, a fence usually needs to be a little more secure, and that's especially in the case of swimming pool surrounds. A very difficult feature to design even in a modern garden, a pool fence will either make or break the ambience and aesthetics of that particular area. I usually try to make the fence invisible, which can be done, for example, by creating a garden area near the pool using dense shrubs. Within that garden I'll install a fence of black metal flat bar that conforms to the standards of the regional authorities. For the gate, the idea is to keep it simple and to have it in a position where, even without the pool, a gate would make sense. Clever landscape design, such as elevating a pool to make it safe, or integrating the design within garden walls, is a resourceful way of getting around the problem.

Maintaining a theme throughout a property will also provide you with a suitable fence design. The fence design around the swimming pool in the garden at Ingleneuk (page 136) was inspired by the detailed timberwork on the house. The lower part of the fence was constructed from tongue-jointed timber palings, while the top open battens were painted in the burgundy and white colour scheme of the house. Commonsense in the garden is required and it is best to use such detailed work only where absolutely necessary.

Fences may also be purely for decoration. At Bronte House (page 104), it was decided that a bamboo fence, inspired by those found in French provincial gardens, would be a lovely way to finish the eastern terrace. Milled from Bronte's own source of bamboo, the fence added a feeling of nineteenth century garden craft, which was matched by natural twig benches from Lord McAlpine's former collection.

HEDGES

A HEDGE IN the garden is an important structural feature rather than just a clipped plant. A hedge can, in many cases, perform the role of a fence or a wall just as well as the real thing and, in more circumstances than not, it will be much cheaper. The most common hedging plants are buxus, conifer and pittosporum. Throughout the world, though, gardeners have discovered that if it can be clipped, it will be hedged. In Australia, one of the most popular hedging plants is the lilly pilly, a common rainforest tree which produces dense growth when exposed to light. In Asia, the orange flowering tecomaria is an ever-present green screen.

Whether or not to use a hedge, and where to place it, depends on the style of garden. Of course, a Renaissance garden wouldn't be a Renaissance garden without some sort of hedging, and it would generally be positioned by projecting it off a room or face of the house. An Arts and Crafts garden is suited to a hedge, albeit a smaller one than that found in a Renaissance garden but usually a more ornate one, for a hedge can be any shape your imagination will allow. I particularly like the domed mounds on the hedge dividing the topiary garden and the forecourt at Haseley Court. It goes without saying that this additional detail should refer back to some feature found elsewhere on the property.

For the ultra-creative gardener, a tapestry hedge is the ultimate. One of the better designs is that at Hodges Barn (page 124); a spectacular mix of yew, ilex and beech, it has colour, texture and seasonal interest. The hornbeam tunnels at Haseley Court (page 76) are also testament to the skills of hedging, but are not something that can be undertaken lightly. The long tunnels surrounding the walled garden at Haseley have been created by planting hornbeam on both sides of a path, and then training the hornbeam over a frame. Over time, they have met in the middle to form a tunnel, and meanwhile the plants are continually clipped to form solid walls of foliage.

CLOCKWISE FROM TOP LEFT: estate fencing and a ha-ha at Rofford Manor; a rose-covered stone wall at Hodges Barn; a dramatically clipped yew hedge around the terrace at Haseley Court.

BIBLIOGRAPHY

Aitken, Richard, *Gardenesque*, The Miegunyah Press, 2004

Appleton, Marc, *California Mediterranean*, Rizzoli, 2007

Buchan, Ursula, *The English Garden*, Frances Lincoln Ltd, 2006

Campbell, Katie, *Icons of Twentieth-Century Landscape Design*, Frances Lincoln Ltd, 2006

The Garden Book, Phaidon, 2000

Hicks, David and Brooks-Smith Suzannah, *Cotswold Gardens*, Phoenix Illustrated, 1995

Historic Houses Trust of NSW, *Lyndhurst, A Brief History*, 1984

Hobhouse, Penelope, *Plants in Garden History*, Pavilion, 1992

Hobhouse, Penelope, *In Search of Paradise*, Frances Lincoln Limited, 2006

Jekyll, Gertrude and Weaver, Lawrence, *Arts and Crafts Gardens: Gardens for Small Country Houses*, Garden Art Press, 1981

Joyce, David (ed), *Garden Styles: An Illustrated History of Design and Tradition*, Pyramid Books, 1989

Kluckert, Ehrenfried, *European Garden Design*, Könemann, 2000

Latreille, Anne, *Garden of a Lifetime, Dame Elisabeth Murdoch at Cruden Farm*, Macmillan, 2007

Llewellyn Smith, Sir H et al (ed), *Reports on the Present Position and Tendencies of the Industrial Arts as Indicated at the International Exhibition of Modern Decorative and Industrial Arts, Paris, 1925*, Department of Overseas Trade, 1927

Moffett, Marian, Fazio, Michael and Wodehouse, Lawrence, *A World History of Architecture*, McGraw Hill, 2004

Mosser, Monique and Teyssot, Georges (ed), *The History of Garden Design*, Thames & Hudson, 1991

Pizzoni, Filippo, *The Garden, A History in Landscape and Art*, Aurum Press, 1999

Rogers, Elizabeth B, *Landscape Design: A Cultural and Architectural History*, Harry N. Abrams, 2001

Ross, Graham (introduced by), *Botanica*, Random House, 1997

Rutledge, *My Grandfather's House*, Doubleday, 1986

Schofield, Leo, *The Garden at Bronte*, Viking, 2002

Taylor, Patrick, *Period Gardens*, Pavilion, 1991

Thacker, Christopher, *The History of Gardens*, Croom Helm, 1979

Thompson, Ian, *The Sun King's Garden: Louis XIV, André Le Nôtre and the Creation of the Gardens of Versailles*, Bloomsbury, 2006

Tinniswood, Adrian, *The Art Deco House*, Mitchell Beazley, 2002

Turner, Tom, *Garden History, Philosophy and Design 2000BC-2000AD*, Spon Press, 2005

Watkin, David, *A History of Western Architecture, Third Edition*, Laurence King, 2000

Wood, Martin, ed., *The Unknown Gertrude Jekyll*, Frances Lincoln Ltd, 2006

Wood, Martin, *Nancy Lancaster: English Country House Style*, Frances Lincoln Ltd, 2005

ACKNOWLEDGEMENTS

A far larger job than anyone ever expected, yet equally rewarding, *Period Gardens* developed from an idea hatched at Murdoch Books, when Diana Hill and Kay Scarlett asked if I would like to write a book about one of my passions as a garden designer. I would like to thank Diana, Kay and Murdoch Books for giving me the opportunity and support to write this book, and, for her exceptional efforts, Leta Keens, without whom the book would not exist.

I would like to thank the owners and tenants of the many properties we visited: Matt and Clare Handbury, Peter and Lisa Fitzsimons, Jeremy and Hilary Mogford, Michael Reed, Benedetta Origo, Paula and Lindsay Fox, Amanda Hornby, John Schaeffer, Fiona and Desmond Haywood, Michael Ball, The Burns family, Dame Elisabeth Murdoch, The New South Wales Historic Houses Trust at Government House and The National Trust at Stourhead.

Many thanks to Simon Griffiths, for his photographic genius in producing some of the best pictures I have ever seen, and to Andrea Healy, for her talents in designing the book.

I would also like to thank my company and family for having the writing of this book become part of their lives, and thank you to my partner, Kate, who endured my continual focus on it with patience and enthusiasm.

Index

A

Acalypha wilkesiana (Fijian fire plant) 13
Agathis robusta (Queensland kauri) 96
Agave americana 97, 117
Agave fruticosa 117
Agave victoria-regina 88, 102, 112
Albert family 172, 181
Alhambra, Granada 23, 177
Alpinia zerumbet (shell ginger) 117
Amaranthus tricolor 'Joseph's Coat' 11
anti-gardens 215
apartments 218
Araucaria columnaris (New Caledonian pine) 102, 117
Araucaria heterophylla (Norfolk Island pine) 97, 117, 189
arboreta 11, 30, 57, 59, 70, 75, 160
architecture 14, 16-17, 30, 32, 33, 112
Art Deco 32-3, 159, 213, 215, 225, 226-7, 237
Arts and Crafts movement 31, 32, 33, 164
    gardens 31-2, 51, 121, 123, 150, 160, 166-7, 248
Asplenium nidus (bird's nest fern) 10
Atkinson, William 30
Australian gardens 31, 89, 189
Australian Roadside, The 32
avenue planting 190-1, 205, 210

B

Baldwin, Beryl 200
Ball, Michael & Diana 203, 204
Balston, Michael 147
bamboo fencing 119, 248
Bambusa balcooa 119
Banks, Joseph 30
barbecues 144
Barcelona Pavilion 35
Bauhaus school 35
begonias 119
benches 70, 78, 134, 167, 208
Betula jacquemontii (white Himalayan birch) 204
birds 204, 209

Blore, Edward 71
Boboli Gardens, Florence 25
Boomerang, Elizabeth Bay 170, 171, 172-85, 243, 244
cloister garden 17, 19, 181-3, 185
Boston ivy 92, 146, 167, 196
botanical gardens 22
    see also Royal Botanic Gardens
Bowman, Dr James 17
Brogan, John 218
Bronte House, Sydney 13, 14, 89, 93, 104-19, 232, 248
Brown, Lancelot 'Capability' 28, 30, 31, 57, 59, 75
Buckingham, Mr (garden designer) 159
Burle Marx, Roberto 35
buxus (box) 39, 52, 78

C

Californian Mission gardens 32, 169, 171, 184-5
campanula 47
Canary Island date palms 117, 181
Canna iridiflora 13
Canna 'Wyoming' 118
Caruncho, Fernando 177
Cedrus deodara 160
Central Park, New York 31
chalksticks 117
Champs Elysées 28
Charles VIII 25
Chateau d'Amboise 25
Chateau d'Anet 25
cherry laurel 75
chess set topiary 78, 80-1, 85
Chinese gardens 23-4
clivia 117
colonial gardens 89, 106, 111, 189, 203, 209
Comfort Hill, Southern Highlands 202-9
Corymbia citriodora (lemon-scented gum) 192
Crowle, William 218, 221
Cruden Farm, Langwarrin 19, 190-201, 210
Cyathea australis (rough tree fern) 10
Cyathea cooperi (tree ferns) 117

D

date palms 117, 181
Davies, Marjorie 203
de Brosse, Salomon 25
de Medici, Marie 25
de Mercoliano, Pacello 25
de Noailles, Charles 33
De Stijl movement 35
Decameron (Boccaccio) 24-5
Deepdene 30
Delano, Billy 83
Dendrobium speciosum 117
deodars 160
Dowling, Laidley 159
Downing, Andrew Jackson 31
Dracaena draco 97
driveways 124, 191, 241
Dughet, Gaspard 59
Dumbarton Oaks, Washington 32

E

Eastern gardens 23-4
Edwardian gardens 121, 123, 166-7
Ellem, David 221
Encyclopaedia of Cottage, Farm and Villa Architecture (1833) 30
English gardens 28, 30-1, 57
English plane tree 160
environment 17, 19, 57
escallonia 39
euphorbias 117
evergreen oak 41-2
exoticism 32, 225, 227

F

Falling Water 35, 215
Farrand, Beatrix 32
fashionable gardens 57
fencing 119, 248

G

Finlay, Ian Hamilton 35, 66
Flitcroft, Henry 60, 71
Florence 25, 39
follies 71, 78-9
Fontainebleau 28
Fox, Lindsay & Paula 172, 177, 183
frangipani 227
French gardens 28, 238
Frucrea furfuracea variegata 117

G

garden design 13, 14, 16, 51, 83
garden furniture 167
    see also benches
garden rooms 39, 42, 78, 84
Gardenesque style 30, 31, 87, 89, 111, 117, 118-19, 225
Gardenia augusta 'Florida' 166
gardening 31, 189
gardens
    dynamic 19, 106
    evolving 57, 77, 106, 200
    history 22-35
Georgian gardens 73, 75, 77, 84-5
geraniums 53
Gothic revival 14, 16, 77, 106
Government House, Sydney 10-11, 13, 106
Grand Tour 28
gravel 84, 108, 237
Greek gardens 22
Gropius, Walter 35
grottoes 66
Guevrekian, Gabriel 33

H

ha-ha walls 147, 150, 155
Handbury, Clare & Matt 41
Hanging Garden of Babylon 22
Haseley Court, Oxfordshire 76-85, 237, 248
Hatfield House 33, 232
hedging 39, 57, 97, 144, 248

H

Hedychium coronarium (white ginger lily) 112
Hedychium greenei (scarlet ginger) 138
hellebores 164
Hicks, David 16-17, 77, 79, 192, 204
Hoare family 59, 60, 66
Hobbsworth, JB 111
Hodges Barn, Glos 124-35, 247, 248
homestead gardens 31, 187, 189, 210-11
house/garden unity 32, 33, 39, 57, 75, 118
hydrangeas 141, 167
Hymenocallis caribaea (spider lily) 13

I

il Tribolo 25
indoor/outdoor lifestyle *see* house/garden unity
Ingleneuk, Neutral Bay 136-45, 166, 167, 232, 242, 244, 248
Innes, Ian 13
Islamic gardens 17, 23
Italian Renaissance gardens 24-5, 28, 39, 238, 248

J

Jacobean gardens 55, 57
Japanese gardens 23-4
jardin anglais 28
Jardin Exotique, Monaco 112
Jekyll, Gertrude 31-2
Jellicoe, Geoffrey 77-8

K

Kiley, Dan 35
kitchen gardens 39, 154, 156-7
Knox, Edward W 93

L

La Foce, Val d'Orcia 40-53, 238
Lady Astor's canal, Haseley 78
lakes 71, 150, 155, 198-9, 200, 204
Lancaster, Nancy 77, 78, 79, 83
Landscape gardens 30, 55, 57, 238

Landscape movement 28
lawns 226, 232
Le Corbusier 35
Le Nôtre, André 28, 53
Lee, Inge 96
lemon-scented gum 192
Lewis, Brendan 112, 117
Lewis, Mortimer 14, 106
Ligorio, Pirro 25
lilly pilly 248
Lindsay, Norah 77
Little Sparta, Scotland 35, 66
Livingston, Morna 41
Lotusland 177
Loudon, John 30-1
Louis XIV 28
Lowe, Georgiana 106, 111, 112
Lowe, Robert 106, 111
Lucas, Clive 96, 137, 138, 143, 244
Lutyens, Edward 31
Luxembourg Gardens 25
Lyndhurst 17, 137

M

Maritime Art Deco 218
McCartney, Andrew 10
McCoy, Michael 117
meadows 75, 78, 85, 232
Medici family 25
Mediterranean style 16
Melianthus major 89
Mesopotamian gardens 22
minimalism 24, 35, 215, 225, 226, 227
Modernism 33, 35, 213, 215, 226-7
Moidart, Southern Highlands 158-67
Mollet family 25, 28
mondo grass 10
monotone 226
Morrice, William 203
Morris, William 31

Morrison, Michael 19, 196, 200
Murdoch, Dame Elisabeth 19, 192, 196, 200
Murdoch, Keith 192
My Grandfather's House 93

N

National Trust 60, 66
native plants 32, 35, 189
natural gardens 28, 160, 215
New Caledonian pine 102, 117
New Zealand flax 13, 89, 111
Niemeyer, Oscar 35
Nile gardens 22
Noguchi, Isamu 35
Norfolk Island pine 97, 117, 189, 232

O

Odyssey (Homer) 22
Olmsted, Frederick Law 31
Ophiopogon japonicus (mondo grass) 10
orchids 117, 119
Origo family 41, 42, 51, 53
outbuildings 210
outdoor entertaining 39, 78, 106, 144
owners 14, 19, 102, 200

P

Page, Russell 28, 57, 75, 77, 79
Palladian style 59, 60, 71
Palladio, Andrea 71
Paradise gardens 23
Paris Expo, 1925 32, 33
parterres 25, 28, 39, 42, 47, 52
paths 99, 108, 158, 238-41
paving 237
    marble 214, 226
    Moorish 185
    stone 166
perennial gardens 13, 51, 89, 102, 117, 166, 196
Pericoli, Niccolò 25

period gardening 14, 16, 17, 19, 83, 89, 97, 154, 181, 218, 229
Persia 22-3
Phoenix canariensis (Canary Island date palm) 117, 181
Phoenix roebelenii (dwarf date palm) 117
Phormium tenax (New Zealand flax) 13, 89, 111
Picturesque gardens 30, 73, 75, 84-5
Pierre de Ronsard (rose) 51
Pinches, Debbie 10
Pinsent, Cecil 41, 42, 47, 53
Platanus x *Hybrida* (English plane tree) 160
ponds 131, 140, 147, 173, 244
pools *see* swimming pools
Potts Point 218
Prunus cerasifera 'Nigra' (purple leaf flowering plum) 13

Q

Queenslander houses 203
Quercus ilex (evergreen oak) 41-2

R

Rann, Bruce 10
Renaissance gardens 24-5, 28, 37, 39, 248
Repton, Humphry 30, 75
retaining walls 16, 160
rhododendrons 75
Ricinus rubra 119
Rofford Manor, Oxfordshire 146-57, 232, 248
Roman gardens 22
romanticism 32, 78, 102, 117, 196
Rona, Bellevue Hill 19, 90-103, 241
roof gardens 35, 218, 221, 225
rose gardens 51, 154, 160, 164, 192, 200
Royal Botanic Gardens, Sydney 10, 13, 59, 106, 209
Rutledge, Helen & Martha 93
Ryoan-ji, Kyoto 24

S

Saarinen, Eero 35
Saint Germain 28
Samuels, Gordon 10
Schaeffer, John 19, 93, 97, 102, 172, 183
Schofield, Leo 13, 14, 19, 60, 106, 111, 117
screening 200
sculpture 50, 68, 70, 98, 102, 204
Senecio serpens (chalksticks) 117
shadow line 215, 222, 225
Shelley, Max 17, 172, 177, 181, 183
Shepherd, Mr (gardener) 78
Shiress, Mr (botanist) 159
shrubberies 73, 75
Silk Road 22-3
Smithsonian Institute 31
Sorensen, Paul 159
Southern Highlands 159, 203
Spanish Mission gardens 32, 169, 171, 184-5
statuary *see* sculpture
stone flagging 166
Stourhead, Wiltshire 59, 60-71, 75, 232, 238, 248
    Pantheon 66, 69
    temples 59, 60, 66, 71
Strelitzia nicolai (giant bird of paradise) 13, 112
succulents 112, 117, 118
swimming pools 143-4, 147, 154, 242, 248
symmetry 84

T

tapestry hedges 127, 248
tennis courts 131, 138, 154, 232, 234-5
terraced (sloping) gardens 159-60
terraces 116, 180, 185, 221, 225
The Grove 204
Thunbergia mysorensis 112
topiary 22, 52, 78, 80-1, 85
travertine marble 53
trees 57, 59, 66, 160, 197, 203, 211

U

Unité d'Habitation, Marseille 35
United States 31, 32, 35

V

Vaux, Calvert 31
vegetable gardens 39, 154, 156-7
Versailles 14, 25, 28, 53, 241
Victorian gardens 11, 87, 89, 111, 117, 118-19
views 30, 53, 78, 85, 97, 102, 144, 164, 197, 232
Villa d'Este, Tivoli 25
Villa I Tatti 41
Villa Lante, Bagnaia 25, 52
Villa Medici 41
Villa Savoie 35
vistas *see* views

W

Walling, Edna 32, 159, 160, 192, 197, 201
walls 16, 147, 150, 160, 194, 207, 247-8
Walska, Ganna 177
Ward, Tony 96
water features 52, 78, 150
    see also lakes; ponds
weeds 119
West Indies 189, 203
White House, Washington 31, 71
Wilkinson, Leslie 16
windbreaks 203, 204
Wood, Martin 83
Worner, Clarrie 160
Wright, Frank Lloyd 35, 215
Wyldefel Gardens, Potts Point 216-27

Y

Yucca elephantipes 97
Yucca filamentosa 13

Z

Zierholz, Martin 10-11, 13

Published in 2008 by Murdoch Books Pty Limited

AUSTRALIA
Murdoch Books Australia
Pier 8/9
23 Hickson Road
Millers Point NSW 2000
Phone: +61 (0)2 8220 2000
Fax: +61 (0)2 8220 2558
www.murdochbooks.com.au

UK
Murdoch Books UK Limited
Erico House, 6th Floor North
93-99 Upper Richmond Road
Putney, London SW15 2TG
Phone: +44 (0) 20 8785 5995
Fax: +44 (0) 20 8785 5985
www.murdochbooks.co.uk

Chief Executive: Juliet Rogers
Publisher: Kay Scarlett
Concept: Sarah Odgers
Designer: Andrea Healy
Editor: Leta Keens
Commissioning editor: Diana Hill
Photographer: Simon Griffiths
Production: Monique Layt

National Library of Australia Cataloguing-in-Publication Data: Baldwin, Myles.
Period Gardens: Landscapes for Houses with History Includes index. ISBN 978 1 74045 906 8 (hbk.)
1. Landscape gardening.   2. Gardens – Design. 712.6

Printed by 1010 Printing International Limited. PRINTED IN CHINA. First printed in 2008.

Cover photo: A mixed planting at the Victorian-style garden of Rona in Sydney combines the
traditional with the exotic. Opposite title: a column of Scottish yew leads to the entrance of Hodges
Barn in Gloucestershire. Opposite contents: a corner of the garden at Rona.